Gym Biz

Starting and Running Your Own Gym For ProFIT

Published by MuscleMag International
5775 McLaughlin Road
Mississauga, ON
Canada L5R 3P7

Canadian Cataloguing in Publication Data

Ravelle, Lou, 1927-
    GymBiz: starting and running your own gym for profit

ISBN 1-55210-019-7

1. Physical fitness centers--Management. I.Title.

GV428.5.R39 2000   338.7'616137   C00-900921-3

Designed by Jackie Kydyk

10 9 8 7 6 5 4 3 2 1 Pbk

Distributed in Canada by
CANBOOK Distribution Services
1220 Nicholson Road
Newmarket, ON
L3Y 7V1
800-399-6858

Distributed in the United States by
BookWorld Services
1933 Whitfield Park Loop
Sarasota, FL 34243

Printed in Canada

Table of Contents

Introduction

One of the most popular stars of the '20s and '30s was Siegmund Klein. With his great shape, thick musculature and extreme definition, Klein set the standard for the next decade or so.

Looking back at well over forty years in the health and fitness business, I have to say that I have seen many changes and innovations, but the biggest change has been in the business itself and in the way that it has expanded.

In the beginning it wasn't a business at all and when I started my first small gym in the west end of London, eyebrows were raised and heads were shaken. More than one friend said something like, "Call that a business?" They were right, of course, at that time it wasn't a means to earn a living, but I did manage to scratch out an existence.

Imagine, there I was right in the heart of the capital and I had virtually no competition at all and yet I found it very hard to keep going. How things have changed and what a different story it is today when even relatively small communities boast a flourishing gym or leisure centre.

The expansion that has taken place has been due to the public's ever-increasing interest in health and fitness. However, I doubt that the interest would have been created if we, that is the pioneer gym operators, had not kept going. Growth in the early days was slow and we received little or no publicity from the press. If we did get a mention it was usually of a derogatory nature, so that didn't help. Still, we forged ahead and slowly the public began to realize the importance of a sound mind in an even sounder body. They began to discover that good healthy bodies were not just the birthright of a lucky few.

Gradually, over the years, people from within the ranks of the physical culture movement began to make it not only a way of life, but also an occupation. A mere handful of hopeful believers struggling to rake in a precarious living, created what has now grown into a thriving profession. A new industry has been born and it is rapidly expanding and creating more opportunities as it does so.

In line with the growing interest in health and physical fitness an ever-increasing number of people are looking to it as their vocational field and it is for these that this book is intended.

Instructors' courses and courses in physical education are available and while the student may come away from these with the necessary knowledge, this in itself will not guarantee success if he/she is planning a career in physical culture.

Running a successful gym, or even teaching in one, requires a very special approach. It's not just having a well-equipped gym, and showing people how to do the exercises or use the equipment. There are several other factors involved and I shall attempt to explain them. In addition to being a teacher or mentor, one also has to know something of the psychological aspect of salesmanship when entering the commercial field. This great new industry is, after all, the commercial side of what was hitherto, a completely amateur domain.

We are talking of a new industry, one in which, up to now, there have been no real guidelines. I hope that, through this book, I can provide some.

Klein convinced many that physical appearance was just as important as physical strength – but with the added benefit of overall good health.

Health and Fitness as a Career

From very small beginnings, the health and fitness movement has grown into a flourishing business. What was, in the early post-war years, a small back-room activity, has now achieved shopping mall status. In the not-too-distant past anyone who spent his spare time in a gym, and heaving iron about, was looked on as a little odd. I know because I was one of those oddballs.

However, some of us soldiered on, I suppose because we knew that we'd discovered something worthwhile – and this crazy pastime grew. (Lots of people began to discover that the 'iron pills' could put a very special quality into life.) Pumping iron became an accepted part of life and health and fitness, and as an industry, was born. It is an industry manned by enthusiasts. The people running, managing and working in gyms and fitness centres all share a deep-rooted devotion to health, fitness and physical betterment.

The fitness boom, which has really gathered momentum over the last two decades, has brought together people from widely differing backgrounds. Worldwide, there are millions of enthusiasts who practice this remarkable self-help activity. People who live and breathe the fitness lifestyle have a common dream, to make their hobby into their careers. There are various possibilities open. Heading the list and the ultimate goal of most, is of course, gym ownership. There are also openings for managers and instructors. Recent years have seen the start of a constantly-increasing demand for 'personal trainers.' These are instructors who give clients exercise in their homes on a one-to-one basis. And there is a growing trend toward the use of 'one on one' trainers in gyms.

If you are one of the above mentioned dreamers, this book can help you to make your aspirations become reality. You may have had ideas of joining the profession for some time.

From very small beginnings, the health and fitness movement has grown into a flourishing business. What was once a small back-room activity, has now achieved shopping mall status.
– Vince Gironda

You've probably had several years of experience on the gym floor and have a good working knowledge of exercise and nutrition. More than likely you have already taken one of the excellent instructor's courses that are now available. All this is great and will stand you in good stead, but it will not, in itself, guarantee you success in your chosen field.

Your success will depend on your knowledge of lots of other factors and also on your whole approach. It is one thing being a member of a gym, or fitness centre (for your own health and well-being), but it's an entirely different situation when you've got to run one – and make it pay.

Once you are dealing with the public, once this fitness and health bug, with which you've been involved for so long, becomes your means of earning a crust, you become a professional. The trouble is that this transition happens overnight and you've got to be prepared, in advance, to look and act like a pro. One of the main objects of this book is to help you to do just that.

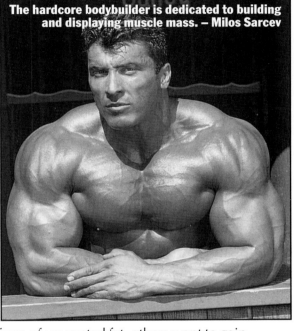

The hardcore bodybuilder is dedicated to building and displaying muscle mass. – Milos Sarcev

You may have already started your career in the gym field, running your own gym, or working in one or as a personal trainer. In any of these cases, there are many factors which can help to make your career more successful. On the other hand you may already be the owner of a successful chain of health clubs. In this case you don't need this book, but you might consider it as essential reading for all your staff.

There are several different types of gyms and at times their functions may overlap, so, let's define just what we have in mind when we talk about a 'health and fitness' set-up.

The fitness gym caters for people who want better bodies and a higher degree of physical fitness. Exercising or training with weights and progressive resistance machines is the way to achieve this. Many of the members are interested in losing weight, in the form of unwanted fat, others want to gain weight. Weight gaining usually takes the form of packing on some useful muscle.

There are also the out and out bodybuilders. This latter group can be subdivided into 'lifestyle' and 'hardcore' categories. Lifestyle means, more or less, what it says. It covers men and women who perform bodybuilding exercises, with weights and machines and get a kick out of the better physical health and the increased quality of life that this activity brings. To the professional these people are his bread and butter.

The hardcore bodybuilder is something else. He, or in some cases she, is completely dedicated to building and displaying muscle mass. The displaying is done at championships and contests and also through the pages of the physical culture press. Hardcore enthusiasts make up the smaller of the two segments of the bodybuilding discipline and as such they are only a small part of overall gym membership. However, we must not overlook their importance. They are the people that get the publicity and help the movement to grow. Think of the publicity and the inspiration to youngsters, stirred up by men like Arnold Schwarzenegger (hardcore, if ever there was) and Sylvester Stallone.

Between the two bodybuilding extremes there is also, what I like to call, a middle-of-the-road category. They are perhaps, more dedicated than the lifestylers, are hooked on bigger muscles, (it's true), but they don't enter competitions.

GYMBIZ

Anyone who contemplates opening a gym must first decide which section of the market is the target area. To my mind the best bet is the lifestyle sector, or perhaps somewhere between lifestyle and middle-of-the-road. That's where the business is. A few people have made it big in the hardcore gym field, but they are the exceptions. Unless you are another Schwarzenegger, or you have a doctorate in muscle growth, forget the heavy mob, (bless 'em). You'll find one or two of them in your gym anyway.

Fitness gyms come under various names. Health Studio, Leisure Centre, Health Club, and Spa are just some of the variations.

Anyone who contemplates opening a gym must first decide which section of the market is the target area.

The other two main types of gym specialize in aerobics and martial arts, though in many instances fitness gyms offer one or both of these activities as extras. The larger 'leisure centres' of course, with their greater size are able to cover a wider range of 'classes' and cater to various other types of activity.

Who are the people that are most likely to succeed in the gym business and which group do they come from?

Well, again I think the lifestylers have it. And again, perhaps a lifestyler with just a dash of hardcore in his muscle tissue. This leads to another important point. You don't need to be a bodybuilding champion to run a successful gym. You don't have to be a muscular giant. It's true that you should have a good, well above average, physique and a healthy appearance. Being too big and muscular can put some people off. Most people feel more at ease if their mentor is not too spectacularly gigantic in appearance.

Joe Public, on his first and all-important visit to the gym, wants to talk to somebody with whom he can identify. If he is greeted by someone with a fifty-four-inch chest, he may feel intimidated. I am not implying that a physique star cannot do well in the gym business. He can, but unless he is running a 100 percent hardcore muscle farm, he'll have to make great changes in his way of thinking and his approach.

The above observations not only apply to gym owners but to anyone working in the gym environment; as managers and instructors. For personal trainers, giving people exercise in their own homes, presenting an image with which the client feels at ease and relaxed is of paramount importance (more about this in chapter 13).

The importance of your approach to, and rapport with, the public, or shall we say your clients or pupils, cannot be overstressed, it is of the utmost importance. The following will serve to illustrate my meaning.

A gym-owner friend of mine in London once engaged a young man as an instructor. He had a good clean-cut athletic physique, nice personality and excellent references. He had also been a physical training instructor in the army. He used his parade ground manner on they paying customers and the result was disastrous. He had to go. You can't treat people who are paying to do something in the same way you treat people who have been ordered to do it.

Few people, when they embark on a career in the fitness field, will have thought of themselves as salespeople. Rather they will have thought of themselves as athletes, teachers and in some cases even gurus (this last one is a mistake). Later, they are often surprised to find that salesmanship is a large part of the job. Very often, when a prospective member enters the gym for the first time, it is because he feels he wants to do something about his physical state. It may seem strange, but he still needs to be sold the idea. If that person is not given the extra push into doing something about it today, he may leave without joining. Experience has shown that people who don't commit themselves to joining on their first visit, more often than not, do not come back.

The health and fitness industry can provide a career that is both satisfying and rewarding.

There is a need for a fairly specialized type of selling. Unlike most other businesses, we are selling something that you can't see, (and can't wrap up in brown paper and take away with you). At best we're selling a promise – better health, or better appearance. What we are selling is wellness and though this is fast becoming a buzz word, it's not something readily visible.

Very often, what the prospective client needs most of all, is assurance and reassurance. He needs to be sure of several things:
1. That he's making the right decision in getting started.
2. That exercise will really work (for him).
3. That he has come to the right place.
And perhaps above all –
4. That you are the person, or people to help him.

Bearing the above in mind, it becomes obvious that your sales psychology must be specially tailored to meet these needs. This is discussed in some depth in chapter 6.

An ever-increasing number of women are entering a career in the health and fitness field. Of these I would ask forgiveness, if I seem to have fallen into the chauvinistic habit of putting everything in the masculine gender. I have only done so out of convenience and in order to avoid that clumsy 'he or she, his/her' business. Almost all of the advice, observation and information in this book applies equally to both sexes.

The health and leisure industry can provide a career that is both satisfying and rewarding. Can you think of a more fulfilling job than helping people to help themselves? This is the reason why this growth industry is staffed, entirely by believers and enthusiasts. They thrive on spreading the gospel.

These ambassadors have to be fed and clothed and the premises that they work in (some modern facilities are nothing short of palatial) have to be paid for and maintained. We have progressed a long way from the dank, sweat and sawdust days and today, even the humblest gyms have their share of chrome and glitter. Quite naturally in the wake of all this progress, commercialism has crept into what used to be a purely amateur area.

In order to survive in the field today, the gym owner has to be businesslike and he has to learn to compete. He may even have to compete with the established giants in his area, but this need not be cause for alarm. The small man can always offer something that the big boys can't. A much more personalized service and, because of his lower overhead, he can usually do this at a better price. He may also find that he gets spin off from the Big Brother's blanket advertising – for free. He can not only survive, he can also flourish.

Location

"I have a dream!"
Martin Luther King made these words famous. His dream was of a world where everyone was equal. The dream of many a health and fitness buff, is of a world where he has his own gym and he's working in the environment he loves. The idea is great and all over the world lots of people have made it come true.

Perhaps you are one of those who are thinking of getting into the business, though you may of course, have already started. Or perhaps you're still thinking, "Who knows, one day ..." Whichever is the case, you may want to examine some of the things that make the gym business tick.

Money Matters

Money, or capital, is of course a consideration, as in any business. However, starting a gym doesn't necessarily have to cost you a fortune. You can start in a modest location and with modest equipment and facilities. If you do this, try to choose a place where facilities and space can be extended at a later date. Remember, provided that you're in the right place, you don't have to try to compete with the giants of the industry and you don't need to have all the latest state-of-the-art, hi-tech goodies. If you must have them and cash is tight, they can come later.

The location of your gym will be one of the key factors in its success.

Remember also, that one area where the small man has the edge on the giants and the franchise gyms is that of really personal involvement. He is Joe Bloggs, local boy and not just a figurehead of some large corporation.

The Right Place

If you're looking for space to set up your gym, you need to find somewhere airy and with good headroom. It doesn't have to be a ground level. One flight of stairs up or down, won't make any difference to your business, but it can mean a huge difference in the rent. You don't need street level window space, like a furniture store. In fact, this can be a drawback, after all you won't have very much that you can display in the windows.

You can, of course, use some window space for advertising and in any case, don't forget that you'll need space for and illuminated sign outside your premises. You've got to show people where you are.

Where

The location of your gym will be one of the key factors in its success. Obviously you want to be in a good area where there are lots of people. This would naturally suggest a town or city centre, but this of course, could bring its own problems. This first of these could be the astronomical rents that are asked for well situated, city centre property, though sometimes you can still find a bargain. On the face of it you may think that parking could be a problem in the centre of a large city, but in reality it's not as bad as it sounds. Don't forget that in any big, bustling city centre, there are many thousands of people who are already there. These people either live there, or more likely, they have come in to do their regular job. They don't have to park; they are already on the spot.

You don't necessarily have to pick a front line property. A secondary position is fine and the rent will be much lower, but make sure that it's easy to find and easy to direct people to, on the telephone. If you're near a well-known landmark you can make full use of the fact. It's great if you can tell a telephone caller, "We're just round the corner from the Godzilla Hypermarket."

Make sure that you pick a spot that is well served by, or in easy reach of, public transport, buses, trains etc. Avoid areas which are too far from main thoroughfares.

A big consideration in city centre trading is the competition. There may already be a well-established gym or health spa in operation. You will have to decide whether or not they really are competitive with the operation that you have in mind. For example, if there is already in operation a luxurious health club with facilities, not only for bodybuilding, but also swimming, jacuzzi, aerobics and squash, you don't have to worry too much. The relatively high price tag that this kind of establishment has to put on its services will ensure that you'll be catering to different levels of the market. I am assuming of course, that you're not planning to start off in the Mega Class yourself, therefore, with your more modest setup, you'll be asking much lower rates. The fact that this other place exists and is much more expensive than yours may even be to your advantage.

If your chosen site is not in a heavily populated area, make sure that you have a good surrounding area, say seventy-five to one hundred thousand people within fifteen minutes driving time. Make sure there's adequate parking. Successful gyms have been run in very small towns, but only when there have been other small towns, or districts, to draw on within that, all-important, fifteen-minute radius. Remember that in the gym business you will always have a revolving or constantly changing membership. Oh, you'll have your nucleus, the "old guard" who stay with you year in year out, but with the rank and file, the drop-out rate is high. This

Take your time, don't make any snap decisions.

means that in order to maintain a healthy membership you must be constantly signing on new people. This is why population is so important.

Thinking about membership brings me to another interesting point. While you are making your preparations, news will get around that you're going to open a gym, this is fine, publicity is what you need. Lots of people, some you've known for a long time and some that you haven't, will say, "You're opening a gym, what a great idea – you've got yourself a client!" Don't set too much store by this and don't be too disappointed when they don't show up. Above all don't push it, you may lose a friend.

Your small friendly gym starts at about 1,500 to 2,000 square feet. A larger square footage, of course, will give you larger scope. I have seen successful gyms with less than this area and though lack of space produces its own limitations, there are flourishing operations with only 1,200 square feet. It will depend on how cleverly you use the space available. The figures above apply to a straightforward fitness/bodybuilding set up. If you want to include other activities, such as aerobics or martial arts (even if this is only an idea in the back of your mind for future expansion) you'll need more space.

Sometimes you find a place which looks ideal but has too many pillars or supporting columns. Don't be put off. This is not as great a drawback as it at first seems. You can deploy your heavy equipment; leg press, Hack machine, Smith machine etc., around these pillars and you won't even notice they're there. Pillars also make ideal fixing points for lat pulleys and crossovers, and other equipment that needs to be securely anchored.

These pillars can also work in your favor. If you moan about the pillars to the landlord you may even get the rent reduced. He already knows all about them and they may be the reason why the place has been on the market as long as it has.

In lots of otherwise likely premises, particularly in basements, there are unsightly pipes running along the ceiling. These can be another stumbling block for the owner or landlord, trying to rent. Again you may be able to get some bargaining power out of this fact and thereby secure a better deal on the rental. Then, if you paint the whole ceiling black or midnight blue and use hooded lighting suspended on chains, you won't even see the ceiling. It will merge into the shadows, taking the pipes with it. This could be an economical alternative to boxing in the offending pipes.

The requirements for a gym differ from most other businesses. You don't need window space, you don't need a view, but you do want open space without walls, for most of the area anyway. Because of this you'll often find yourself looking at places that other businesses wouldn't even consider. Sometimes, I know from experience, you can strike a great deal on one of these "white elephants."

Old movie theatres, used car showrooms and even old churches, have been turned into successful health and fitness studios. And very often these places are hard to let and high on the white elephant list. All that is needed is a little imagination.

It's as well to bear the above in mind when making the rounds of real estate agents, in your quest for the ideal premises. I have found that often, if you say that you're looking for somewhere to use as a gym, you are immediately told that they have nothing like that on their books. The trouble is that when they hear the word gym it may conjure up a mental picture of the old school gym hall and true enough, the average property agent won't have too many of those on the books. In any case the lofty, uninviting old school gym image is just what you're trying to avoid.

It is a better plan to stress, in the first place, the approximate size you are looking for and make it clear that you are not in search of an institutional type property or even a hall. Make it clear that what you are looking for is X square feet of space with good headroom and it must be in a suitable area.

In considering any premises, the rental asked will be one of the key factors affecting your decision. You will have to weigh the size or capacity of the place and your estimated turnover against the rent being asked. This is not easy to do as your estimated turnover will be something of an imponderable. If you have any doubts you can consult somebody else already in the business. Ideally he would be in another region or town but his counsel could be invaluable in trying to calculate your projected turnover.

Take your time, don't make any snap decisions. You may not find the ideal location immediately, but if you keep looking, the right one will turn up.

The Layout

When considering a premises as a suitable site, you must have in your mind, some idea of what the eventual layout will be. The layout will be governed by several factors.

• The exact type of facility you intend to provide. Will your clientele be men, women, or both? Are you offering sauna? Are you planning a juice bar?

• Are you planning to have a separate area for aerobics and/or martial arts?

• The type of equipment you plan to install, weights, machines etc.

• The physical shape of the place and how it lends itself to the factors above (this one sounds like a chicken and egg situation).

Let's look at the first of these three, this business of the sexes. Most gyms and centres nowadays, cater for both sexes as it obviously makes for a larger market. If you are thinking of doing this, another question arises. Are you planning two separate exercise areas, one for each sex, or will the gym floor be mixed? I have found that gyms that have separate facilities for men and women, have a much higher percentage of female membership than those that are co-ed. Sometimes, where this separation is practiced, I have noted that women make up as much as 50 percent of the total membership. (Seems that while some ladies don't mind sharing with the men, others do prefer to be segregated.) Many mixed gyms only report 10 percent or less, female membership.

FIGURE 3.1 Unisex Gym

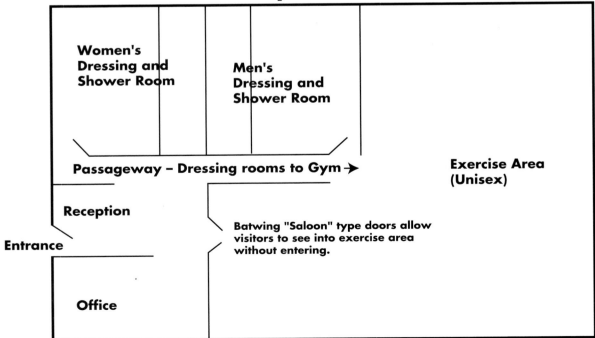

Women's Dressing and Shower Room

Men's Dressing and Shower Room

Passageway – Dressing rooms to Gym ➜

Exercise Area (Unisex)

Reception

Batwing "Saloon" type doors allow visitors to see into exercise area without entering.

Entrance

Office

FIGURE 3.2 Separate Gyms

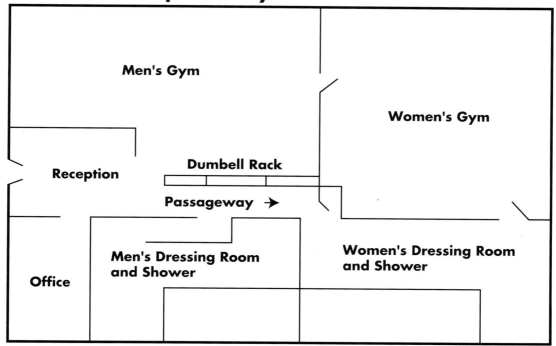

In either case if you have both sexes using your facility, you'll need male and female shower rooms. At this stage it is well to remember to plan your layout so the two shower rooms are back to back, or side by side. You will be able to make use of the same plumbing for hot water and drainage. This can mean big savings.

Separate exercise floors mean more space and equipment required, so whether or not you do this will, of course, depend largely on your budget.

The matter of equipping the gym is dealt with in the next chapter, but obviously anyone who is looking at premises will have some idea of how he wants to equip the place. With some of the bigger machines, it's just as well to know in advance the floor measurements of these pieces. This helps you to decide whether or not a certain piece of equipment will fit in a given corner or alcove. More on this in chapter 4.

Next you have to consider the shape or configuration that you have to work with. Take time and plan out roughly where your various departments will fit in, without too much alteration and pulling down of walls. If the layout of the premises does not quite lend itself to the plans you originally had in mind, but in spite of this you like the place, possibly because of its location, or shape, you may change your way of thinking. It's good to be flexible.

When you are doing your first inspection of a likely premises, one of the things you should bear in mind is that you will need a reception area with a small office where you can interview prospective members. This is one of the most important success factors and its value

Figure 3.2 shows a layout for men and women in two separate gyms. Note that the shower areas are end to end, thus making use of the same water supply and drainage runs. Note also the positioning of the dumbell rack to form a "natural" passageway to the women's dressing room. Instead of a dumbell rack, a similar effect could be obtained by an arrangement of machines or other equipment to form this walkway.

FIGURE 3.3
Sauna Solution

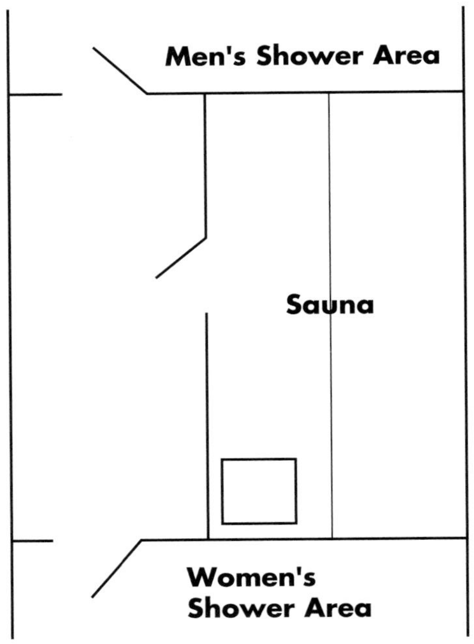

Men's Shower Area

Sauna

Women's Shower Area

Figure 3.3
Instead of installing separate saunas for men and women, a single unit can be used as shown here.
The appropriate doors can be locked or unlocked on the designated days.

cannot be over-emphasized. The office, or interviewing area, is so important and the size of your membership will depend so much on how you make use of it, that it rates a whole chapter to itself.

If you are considering a prospective location, don't forget the above points. Try to choose the solution that doesn't lead to a big remodeling job. If there is a fair amount of modification and rebuilding to be done, don't be afraid to ask for, say, a 3-month rent-free period on the grounds that it's going to take you that long to put the place in shape. This ploy often works, especially when the place needs a face-lift anyway. It's well worth a try.

When thinking out the layout, dressing room space has to be taken into consideration. Sometimes the proposed premises will have various rooms, which can be utilized for this without too much modification. If this isn't the case and you are dealing with a more open plan area, dressing areas can often be formed by the use of fairly lightweight partitioning. This has several advantages over the more traditional methods of room division, i.e. bricks, or cinder blocks and mortar. It is cheaper, quicker, less messy and often within the capabilities of a handyman rather than a skilled, and more expensive tradesman. However, a word of caution is called for here. Materials used should be fire resistant. If you are contemplating using materials that are non-fire resistant, check with your local authority first. They won't necessarily ban the use of certain materials, but they may specify that you treat them with fire retardant paint, or something of the sort. Or, they may place a limit on what percentage of your partitioning may be made up of these materials. They may even suggest alternatives.

These city hall gentlemen can appear very inflexible at times and it doesn't pay to rub them up the wrong way. In the process of starting your business, you may have to deal with several of them, from different departments. Be patient. They may put up, what seems to be an insuperable barrier to something that you had in mind. However, there's usually a legal way around it which will keep both of you happy.

The dressing rooms themselves should be kept simple and easy to clean. Really, all that they need contain is long benches and hooks on the walls for hanging clothes. You can install lockers, or cubbyholes for clothes, but though this helps to dress the dressing room, it also brings its own attendant problems. Installing lockers may provide extra revenue as they can be rented out on a monthly basis. It sounds good but it's loaded with drawbacks. What happens, for instance, when somebody who has rented the locker for a month, drops out and is never seen again. First, you don't even know for sure that he's dropped out. He may have simply taken a holiday, so the locker remains firmly locked, probably with a smelly old towel and a pair of gym shoes inside. If and when you do discover, or decide, that he has dropped out and is not just taking a short lay-off, you might think about re-renting the locker. Can you open it, or has he got the only key? If you do open the locker, what do you do with any gear that may be inside?

In my experience the amount of control and policing required may not be worth the small income that can be derived. I think it's better not to have lockers, or the hassle that they entail and give members more room to change. I know that a lot of people will disagree with this, but I have learned the hard way that you're just better off without them and all the problems that they can produce. Some members may complain about lack of locker facilities, but I don't think you'll lose any clients over this. You can point out that as most people come by car, it shouldn't be a problem to stow their sports bag in the trunk. Finally, if you really can't live without lockers – rent them on a daily basis only.

You must however, make some sort of provision for security. By this I mean the security of the members' valuables while they are actually training. The simplest method is to suggest, or insist, that they be handed over to the management for safe keeping. There should be notices to this effect in the reception area and also in the dressing rooms.

When looking at a prospective premises, you'll have to divide it up, mentally at first and later on paper, to see how it lends itself to your gym concept. There are certain factors that are important and should be kept in mind, these are listed below.

• Entrance.
You will need an entrance hall or reception area. If space is tight, this needn't be very large. Your office, as discussed elsewhere, should lead straight off the reception area, or be very close to it.

• Dressing Rooms
Ideally, these should be located so that members do not have to cross the gym floor in their street clothes, in order to change. If this is not possible, try to minimize the amount of gym floor they have to cross.

• Separate Gyms
If you are thinking of separate gyms for men and women, try to arrange things so that one sex won't have to walk across the gym-floor of the other, to reach their own territory. While the men won't object to this, I know that some of the girls find it a little off-putting. No. 3.2 shows an effective way of dealing with this problem. Note the use of a passageway formed partly by machines and equipment.

Once you have reached the stage of deciding what will go where, it is worthwhile making some sort of a plan on paper. Very often the property agents, or the owner of the premises, will be able to supply you with a plan. If not, it is not too difficult to make a rough one with the aid of a tape measure and a pencil and paper. A scale of say, 1/4 inch to the foot for the purpose of making this preliminary sketch. The idea at this stage, is to see how best you can make use of the available space and how best you can lay out the equipment you have, or have in mind.

Try to arrange things so that the most impressive or spectacular looking equipment, will be displayed to the greatest advantage. Usually, this will mean close to the entrance and not tucked away in a corner.

It is important not to make the mistake, unfortunately seen all too often, of over-equipping the exercise area. Your members need room to move.

Equipment

The equipment in any gym or health centre, should be chosen with great care. Bear in mind that it will not only be used to create physical development, but also that its very appearance can have a positive effect on people. For this reason the equipment should not only be functional, it must look good.

In the late forties and early fifties, when the first of the new breed of exercise machines came on the scene, their designers, enthusiasts themselves, were mainly interested in the function and performance of the apparatus. Little attention was paid to aesthetics and looks. These results were sometimes pretty monstrous and the machines often had a torture chamber look. When the fitness movement exploded and became an industry, designers were called in and the machines developed much more pleasing lines.

The first thing a would-be-member sees when he enters the gym is the equipment. Make sure that what he sees is impressive and inspiring. Your equipment is part of your showmanship and if it looks right it can inspire in people, that "can't-wait-to-get-started" feeling.

All of your gym equipment should be chosen with great care. It should look impressive and inspiring.

Photo courtesy of Gold's Gym, Venice, CA

Free weights are virtually indestructible. They can last forever.

Photo courtesy of Gold's Gym, Venice, CA

The way you actually equip the gym will be governed by various factors, not the least of which will, of course be cash – how much you want to spend. In an ideal situation, the sky would be the limit, and the new gym would be filled with glittering, beautifully matched, state-of-the-art machinery. However, many people starting out in business look for ways to economize. It makes sense to keep some capital in reserve, rather than spend it all at the beginning.

Free weights are virtually indestructible, they last forever. A coat of paint once in a while and they are indistinguishable from new. This makes a strong case for buying free weights second hand. Most good quality exercise machines are built to last a lifetime and can often be picked up, second hand, at a fraction of their initial cost. With a bit of paint and possibly new cables they will be as good as new. A tiny ad in the classified columns of your local newspaper can produce great results in the search for used equipment. If some of the material you buy is not exactly what you would have liked, you can always upgrade at a later date. See chapter 8 for more information on this aspect. Of course, if money's no object and you really want to start off with a big bang – go ahead, buy new.

The bench press is just about the most popular single exercise. You'll need at least two bench press stations, one light and one heavy. The same goes for squat racks, plan for two sets at least. You'll need a full range of dumbells and barbells, graduated in five and ten pound stages respectively. It's also a good idea to have duplicates at the lighter end of the weight range. More about this later.

At some stage during your planning you will have to decide on what percentage of your hardware will be in the form of traditional free weight-training equipment and how much of it will be mechanized. Don't forget that the free weight equipment must include benches, stands and racks and allow for this when mapping out your space.

If you are planning on having at least some serious bodybuilders, either hardcore or middle of the road, you will have to have a fairly comprehensive range of free weights. It doesn't matter how many glittering high-tech machines you have, these boys won't be happy unless they can hoist some real iron. And they've got a point too, really there is no substitute for free weights. Most machines, with only one or two exceptions, are only substitutes for free weight exercises.

Where free weights have the edge over machines is that you have to control them. If you are doing, say, a bench press on a machine, the bar can only move in two directions – up or down. With weights the bar is free to move in any direction, backward, forward or sideways. In fact you have to control it through 360 degrees. Because of the amount of control required, you get much better results in the way of development and quality. The amount of control required when using a pair of dumbells, as opposed to a barbell, is even greater.

A fine display of machines looks good and helps you sell the gym.

Photo courtesy of Gold's Gym, Venice, CA

However machines have their purpose. They are comfortable, easy to use and with the modern weight stacks, it's so easy to change the poundage. Machines are particularly useful for people doing rehabilitation exercises when recovering from accidents and for this reason you will see them in hospitals.

Above all, a fine display of glittering machines looks good and this helps you to sell the gym. Yes, even experienced iron pumpers are sold by machinery, even though they may rarely use it. It seems they like to see it around.

Gym and leisure centre owners like to see it around too and I think it's safe to say that the advent of this gleaming generation of exercise machinery has played a major part in the boom in the health industry that has taken place in the last decade or so. The beginner, using a machine for the first time needs almost no special instruction. He just puts the pin in the right hole to select the recommended weight and then pumps out the required number of repetitions. What could be easier?

Beginners often are, placed on routines which are almost, if not entirely, made up of mechanized movements. I'm not sure that I entirely approve of this, perhaps because it sounds too much like conveyor belt fitness.

When considering the purchase of machines, what should be the priorities? First and foremost an exercise machine should do the job it's supposed to do. Most professional machines are intended for one exercise and one exercise only, beware of multipurpose gadgetry. The only way to be sure that the machine is well designed to fulfill its intended purpose, is to try it out yourself. It has to work smoothly, it has to be comfortable and above all the movement has got to feel right.

Next look for soundness of construction. Strong neat welding and no sharp edges or protrusions on which your members might impale themselves. Comfortable seats of course are a must. The diameter of the pulleys used is another important and often overlooked point. The larger the pulley, the longer the cable will last. A three and a half to four inch diameter should be considered minimum. Incidentally, when buying this type of equipment, make sure that you can get replacement cables, sooner or later you're going to need them. Some ultra modern machines use a fancy kind of flat rubber belting in place of the more traditional steel cables. These machines have beautifully smooth action and are a joy to use. If you are thinking of buying this type of apparatus, make sure that replacement belts are available.

User friendliness must also be considered. Are the adjustments for height and angle etc. easy to make? Really friendly machines even have the weight stack where you can reach it without leaving your seat. On others you may have to unstrap yourself and march round to the other side of the stack just to change the weight.

When buying machinery, make sure it's good solid professional equipment made for constant use in a gym. Beware of flashy, cheap and nasty machines offered in supermarkets and mail order catalogs. They may be okay for home use but will not stand up to the rigors of gym use. They are usually made of very light gauge tubing, chosen not only to reduce manufacturing costs, but also to reduce transport charges. Often too, you'll find that the movements performed on these machines don't have a satisfying feel. This is because they are badly designed and the movements themselves and/or angles are not correct.

Which are the most important machines, the ones that should get priority if say, space, or cash is at a premium? Number one on the list must be the overhead pulley or lat machine as it's often called. I think the lat pulley must have been the forerunner of all modern gym machines. I certainly think it's one of the most valuable.

Next in order of importance, I'd rate the leg extension and leg curl machines, both used for thigh development. Nowadays these two movements are done on separate machines but these are second generation versions of the dual purpose ones which were born in the fifties.

Then there's the Smith machine. This is a kind of bench press apparatus which uses a real bar. It too, goes back a long way.

The leg press machine is another oldie which is still going strong. Not quite a substitute for squats with free weights, but much more comfortable – hence its popularity. That's a point, you want machines that are popular and therefore, are going to be used. It's no good having equipment that just sits there and looks pretty.

When buying machinery, make sure it's good, solid, professional equipment made for constant use in a gym.

You have just got to have a pec-dek. Why? Well, we can lay the blame on Hollywood. Everyone has seen a pec-dek or two on the films. Hardly a picture goes by these days without a scene where the hero, or heroine, in designer training gear, is found squeezing out a few reps on the pec dec. How things have changed since the days of Cagney and Edward G.

The pec-dek is a popular and well designed machine. The manufacturers' design uses the correct angles to give the pectorals a satisfying crunch. The cross-over pulley is also very effective for this area, the only drawback is that it is very space consuming, being about ten feet wide.

High and low pulley are also good investments, used for triceps and dorsal movements respectively.

A standing calf machine will also be heavily used and it is certainly much more comfortable than the old fashioned calf raise. I can still feel the bar digging into my trapezius as my toes fight for purchase on a wobbly block of wood. I would say that the calf machine is one of the few examples where modern technology has come up with a substitute that is better than the original exercise.

Another and more recent addition to the machine arsenal and one which is very popular with the ladies, is the thigh adductor. This machine works the adductors on the inside of the thigh. These muscles are difficult to get at otherwise and many women see the inner thigh as one of their main problem areas.

The above machines should, in my opinion receive preference in your planning. Of course there are lots of others but you will find that though some of these may look spectacular, in fact, as mentioned earlier, they don't get used much.

Before settling on your purchases of equipment it's a good idea to plan things out on paper, as described in the previous chapter. Use little squares of paper, cut to scale to represent the various pieces of equipment and you can shuffle them around on your plan. Make sure that they all fit and leave elbow and walking room. It's all too easy to fall into the trap of over-equipping. I have seen gyms so over-packed with machinery, that the effect is claustrophobic.

Reading the above, it will be obvious that you have to choose equipment that is not only efficient and sturdy in construction, but also good looking. Some manufacturers have managed to combine efficiency and quality with spectacular appearance. This of course, is often reflected in the price, but we can't overlook the sheer impact and therefore sales value, of some of the really impressive, space-age hardware that is on offer at the present time.

I have not mentioned stationary bicycles in the above list because we are really discussing weight stack machines at this point. One or two good bikes are a must, more if you have the room. If you are planning on bicycle classes to music, such as Spinning, then of course you'll

Don't over-equip your gym.
It can feel claustraphobic.

need a whole gang of bikes, say eight or ten. There are many different makes on the market and lots of these incorporate all sorts of electronic wizardry, the choice is yours. Again as with other equipment, it's essential to go for a sturdy professional model, many of the lightweight mail order jobs on offer, wouldn't last a month in a moderately busy gym.

In addition to "moving part" machinery you will need a chinning bar, dipping bars (short parallels) and various benches, both flat and incline. These can all be purchased ready made, though many gym owners get them manufactured to their own specifications. Box section steel tube is the basis of most of the designs and they can be fabricated quite cheaply. Small light engineering firms are usually willing to undertake this kind of work. There is more information on this in chapter 8.

When buying free weights, that is plates, bars and collars you may as suggested earlier, pick up some second hand ones. If you purchase a mixture of new and used equipment, ensure the plates and bar are compatible. This may sound silly but there is more than one size of bar in use. By far the most popular however, is the one inch diameter bar and this is what you should go for.

For general exercise purposes, presses, curls, rowing motions etc., the five foot bar is the most useful length. For bench pressing and squatting, the six foot bar is more suitable. All bars should be chromed or stainless steel, don't accept any that are not. You want your gym to look shiny, not rusty.

When buying free weights, ensure the weights are compatible with the bar.

Photo courtesy of Gold's Gym, Venice, CA

In order to avoid having to have too many loose plates, which you'll eventually find scattered all over your floor, it's a good plan to have as many fixed bars as possible. Ideally a range from ten or fifteen pounds in ten pound increments up to about a hundred pounds. If your weights are in kilos you can think in terms of five to fifty kilos for round figures. It is also a good idea to have one or two duplicates at the lower end, the beginners' end of the scale.

You will need racks for stacking these bars when not in use. They can be stacked horizontally or vertically. I prefer vertical stacking as it takes up less floor space and it makes for easier and safer handling of the bars. Ideally these racks are wall anchored, but if wall space is not available they can be of the free-standing variety. These are usually double-sided and they hold twice the number of barbells for a given length.

Your dumbell range should go from two pounds to at least fifty, in increments of five pounds or two kilos. If you are catering for the real big boys, your dumbell range will have to be extended. The dumbells will be in horizontal racks.

Mirrors are essential equipment.
– Craig Titus

The squatting and bench pressing stations should each have a fixed weight six foot bar in the stands and some spare discs handy so that the poundage can be increased as necessary.

So far we have only discussed ordinary exercise barbells and dumbells. An Olympic bar is much different. It has a diameter of 28 mm and big 50 mm revolving sleeves at the ends. The plates have a large, 50 mm clear holes and of course cannot be used on ordinary bars.

The Olympic bar, though designed for competitive weightlifting, is often found in fitness and leisure gyms. Almost exclusively, in these circumstances it is used as a heavy bench pressing bar. Its extra length gives it a bit more whip than an ordinary exercise bar and once the user has learned the rhythm he can make use of this and do repetitions with higher poundages.

With its big wagon wheel sized 35 or 45 pound discs, it is quite an impressive monster and this makes the Olympic bar popular with the bigger and stronger members. It also can act as an incentive to the not-so-strong, giving them a milestone, or goal to aim for in the future. An Olympic set is definitely an asset. If it fits into the budget – go for it.

Mirrors are essential equipment. Apart from pandering to the narcissistic and enabling you to see what you're really doing, they make the place look bigger and brighter. They also multiply the equipment and the members and so make the place look busier. It is difficult to have too many mirrors, especially full length ones, but here I would like to give a word of warning. Don't be tempted to fit your mirrors right down to the floor or skirting board level. Leave about eighteen inches of wall showing under the mirrors. The reason is this; dumbells, if put down carelessly, have a habit of rolling. If they roll up against a mirror – bingo, end of mirror. On the other hand, if a runaway dumbell only hits the wall, it's just a matter of a lick of paint. A five foot mirror mounted as above will still provide a head to toe image, even if you stand close up.

The health and fitness business has one advantage over lots of other enterprises in that, though the initial setting up and equipping costs are considerable, because of the need for quality equipment, this can be considered a one-time expense. With this in mind, your equipment should be the best your budget will allow.

It's a good plan to have as many fixed bars as possible.

Staff, Image & Professionalism

From the minute that you become a gym operator, manager or instructor, you'll be a professional. It may take you a little time to get used to the idea, but that's how the world will see you. You must act like a pro. Don't forget that you are now in a goldfish-bowl type of job and people will be constantly looking at you.

Why shouldn't they be looking at you? They've come along because they want to better thenselves physically and you're the one that's going to show them how to do it. In view of this, it's easy to see why your image, and that of anyone working with you, is so important. Your members, or pupils, will look to you for an example. You may find that there are some who will watch and even copy, what you eat, if they see you in a local resaurant.

Members will copy what you and your staff do in the gym, so you must always set a good example. (Smoking of course, should not be tolerated anywhere inside your doors. This applies equally to staff and members.)

Let's take a closer look at the question of staff. For many gyms, particularly small ones, it may not be a question in the beginning. Many gyms are run by two partners, or a husband and wife team. This can work very well until they reach the point where they find that the business has grown to proportions where extra help is an unavoidable necessity.

All staff must be enthusiasts. For this reason the best potential recruiting ground is the gym floor. You could go to your nearest job centre and tell them you're looking for a gym instructor or instructress, but you shouldn't expect too much in the way of results. I have found from experience, that while it is possible to contact suitable people through advertising in the press, you'll find the best material right there where you do your own exercise.

You want your staff to be enthusiastic about exercise and training and that they don't simply see it as a job.

An instructor must be interested in people and in helping them.

Models: Frank Cassavetes and Ricardo Avala Photo courtesy of Gold's Gym, Venice, CA

You want someone who is enthusiastic about exercise and training, someone that doesn't just see it as a job. A good personality and ability to mix and adapt are essential. An instructor must be interested in people and in helping them. You want someone who gets satisfaction out of passing on knowledge.

You may find somebody who is the personification of all the above, but lacks a quality that I haven't yet mentioned. That is, the ability to put his own training second to that of the members.

This is probably the biggest single failing of gym instructors the world over. It's true that they have to train themselves, in order to keep in shape, but the members must come first. Some harsh gym operators will not permit staff to do their own exercise during working hours. If they want to train they have to do so when they are off duty. I don't think it is necessary to go to these extremes. I think it is sufficient if their personal training is restricted to those dead, off-peak periods, when there's nobody around that needs attention. A one-hour workout may be spread over several hours, this may not be ideal, but one will get there just the same.

The above advice also applies to the boss; he may well find that he has to take his training where he finds it. A couple of sets of curls here – a set of bench presses there. Don't worry, you won't wither away. It is an acknowledged fact that irregular training can be very beneficial. Many people have taken courses and have certificates and diplomas, which say that they are qualified instructors or trainers. This should be taken into account, but need not necessarily be the deciding factor when choosing staff. A knowledge of anatomy, physiology and exercise, does not in itself, prepare the possessor for dealing with the public. This requires a special personal touch and an understanding of people that would be extremely difficult to acquire from any certificate course.

Let's take a look at what the instructor (and again, this could be the Boss Man himself) has to do while he's on the gym floor.

In the case of a beginner, he will have assessed the new pupil's needs and will have made out a routine for him. Now he will take him through it, demonstrating each new exercise and then inviting the pupil to have a go. On subsequent visits he may not have to demonstrate but he'll be there standing over and supervising, to see that the movements are being done correctly and that the pupil is doing the movements in good style and is not trying to use too much weight. The instructor will give advice on posture and make sure that breathing is correct. Sadly, the last point is one that is often overlooked. Above all, of course, the instructor is there to give encouragement.

GYMBIZ

So far everything is quite straightforward. The pupil has a routine of seven to ten exercises and after three or four sessions he has settled down well. He has been told that he will be on this beginners' schedule for say eight or twelve weeks. He is doing all the exercises perfectly and he has been told that in the weight exercises he should increase the poundage whenever he feels he can, without sacrificing style for weight.

The trouble is, in many gyms, from this point on, our novice is left pretty much on his own. New members have joined and the instructor has to initiate them, as a result, our man can be easily forgotten. The new boy may get the idea that he is being neglected and he may be disenchanted with the whole thing. It's not the kind of publicity you want.

This situation is easily avoided. All the instructor has to do is periodically check to see that his pupil is okay, giving the odd word of encouragement. Two or three times during the workout are all that's needed. It's important to show that you're interested in his progress. He will go away and tell people how they really look after you at that gym. Don't forget to see that he is taken off that beginners' routine at the end of the allotted time. I remember a case once when an instructor overlooked a particularly shy guy and he was left on the beginners' routine for a whole year.

Working in a gym, much of the day will be spent talking. I don't just mean talking about exercise and diet. I mean talking about almost anything and everything, so you've got to be a good listener. Members will tell you much of their life history. If you are working on the gym floor and a member tells you that he has a sister studying medicine, or a brother in the Air Force, remember it. When, a couple of weeks later you ask about his brother or sister and how they are doing, he will know that you are interested and that he is not just another face in the crowd.

A good instructor will give advice on posture and make sure that the breathing is correct.

Dress is very important. Male instructors should wear sweat suits, or dark sweat suit pants and a t-shirt. Or, instead of a t-shirt a crisp white shirt, makes an acceptable and smart alternative. Instructresses can dress like this too, or in tights and leotard. But please, (and I have actually seen it) no high heels.

Anybody working in the front office, or reception area shouldn't be dressed in sports gear. People stepping in from the street feel more at home if they are greeted by someone dressed more or less as they are. As stressed elsewhere, many people that come through your doors only do so after much "plucking up of courage." They don't want to feel out of place, or in any way inadequate or intimidated, so their initial contact on entry is very important. Many feel that they are taking a big plunge into another world so handle with care.

Models: Frank Cassavetes and Ricardo Avala Photo courtesy of Gold's Gym, Venice, CA

A gym member once told me that he actually came to the door of the gym five times before he summoned up sufficient courage to enter. He did enter and he became a convert. Not only did he build a fine physique; he also found self-assurance and lost his shyness. He eventually became an instructor and later opened his own gym. I've seen lots of people undergo this personality change after taking up physical culture, but I always get a feeling of great satisfaction every time I witness it.

The ideal person to be a representative on the gym floor, and that's what an instructor is, would be somebody with a good personality, a good listener and himself, well-spoken and articulate. A good sense of humor is essential. Add to this a likeable manner and a pleasingly athletic appearance and you've got quite a guy – or gal.

Where are you going to find such a paragon? Well as I said, look around you, a dedicated exercise buff is already halfway there, now you've got to make sure that he has the other qualities named above.

When making your choice remember that once they start using your facility,

Instructors should periodically check to see that the members are okay, giving the odd word of encouragement.

your members will probably have much more contact with the instructor, than they will with management. Remember that they are your emissaries, the people you'll be relying on to spread the gospel, so choose well.

As a professional, insist that all members, when on the gym floor, are properly dressed in suitable training gear. No bare feet, a practice that is unhygenic and highly dangerous and no bare chests – I'm thinking of the men's section, of course. It may seem unnecessary to mention this about clothing, but it is very important. I have seen people turn up for training dressed in gardening gear. You've got to step in and correct this sort of thing as it can downgrade your whole operation.

Insist that all weights are put away after use and also that weights are not rested on upholstered benches. You want the gym to always look shiningly new and clean, torn Naugahyde won't help to produce this effect.

Suppose your dream gym is all set up and ready to go, all you need now is lots and lots of contented members to turn your vision into a real success. In other words you now have to consider ways of selling your product to the public. In the gym and fitness business, you are offering, or selling, a service. This service is something that you can't see, feel or touch. For this reason, in order to sell this service, you need to examine the psychological side of things. Particularly with regard to how you present your service. We'll take a closer look at this in the next chapter.

Sales Psychology

It is impossible to over-emphasize the importance of sales psychology. If you get this right it will boost your membership and turn your dream gym into a lucrative career. Overlook it and you could find yourself wondering why the competition has overtaken you.

We are in a unique business. After all, what are we selling? Well, this is where it differs from most other businesses. We're selling something that's invisible. As mentioned earlier, you can't see it, nor can you eat it. You can't wrap it up in brown paper and take it away. Perhaps the whole thing is just a myth, because really we are selling time, space and a promise. To this list you might add, expertise and use of equipment. These very intangibles are what make the business different from most others.

As an example, take some average business, say, a car wash or a shoe repair kiosk. You're in a good location, you have a good installation and you give good service at the right price. There's every chance of success.

In the gym business things can turn out a little differently. You can have a splendid location, well decorated and with wonderful equipment and facilities, not to mention your own personality, of course. Yet, with all this going for you, you can still fall by the wayside. What you must have is a working knowledge of the psychological side of the business. This is a service business, like the two examples named above and like these you're selling a result. Unlike the car wash and the kiosk it's a result that can't be seen – at least not the same day. As I said earlier, you're selling a promise.

First Impressions

Right now there are many people out there who are toying with the idea of doing something about their physical state, many of these, probably for the first time in their lives. Sooner or later they may wander into your studio and ask about joining. At this point, whether a prospect joins or not, depends entirely on what he sees and hears. What he wants to hear, more than anything else, is assurance that he'd be doing the right thing, assurance that you can really help him and in some cases, assurance that no one will laugh at, or try to intimidate him. This last one is something that he'll never come right out and put into words – you have to detect it. In short, he has to hear what he wants to hear.

Making a good first impression is very important.

Models: Kim Lyons and Jesse McCullum

He also has to see what he wants to see. Now this applies not only to the actual installation, but also to the people that he comes into contact with on this all-important first informative visit. Whoever is manning the reception area, and in the average smaller owner-run gym this might well be the owner, should be fully dressed, like anybody in any other office. Your underweight or overweight prospect can be put off right at the start if confronted by a grinning Adonis, all T-shirt and biceps, with a Denver Clamp handshake. Though he may meet some of these once he gets started – now is not the time.

The Tour

After the initial greeting and handshake, you introduce yourself, ask how you can be of service and lead on straight into a tour of the facilities. By the way, be on your guard – he may give you that bone-crushing handshake in order to impress you, it's one of the hazards of the game.

While showing him around the facilities and particularly, the exercise area, you explain the various pieces of

Give a tour of the facilities and explain the different equipment and their useage.

Models: Kim Lyons and Jesse McCullum

equipment and their functions. Do this in an unhurried way, let him ask questions. Try to learn a bit about him while gaining his confidence.

The Interview

The tour eventually leads back to the front office where you and the prospect sit down face to face. The preceding five words are in italics because I want to stress the fact that the interview must be conducted seated, face to face, in an office, or at least an alcove set aside specifically for this purpose. This may seem a trivial point, but it is of the greatest importance. You will lose members if you try to do this interview standing up. This point is dealt with in greater depth in Chapter 7 (The Office).

You ask the prospect what his aims are, and when he tells you, again you must give him that reassurance that he has come to the right place and that he will be doing the right thing. After this you explain the opening hours etc. Let him agree that the hours you offer fit in with his timetable. Next you talk about the actual exercises he will be doing and finally you reach the price structure, membership rates etc. There is a reason for this order. If you mention the rates first, you may find that when you come to the hours, he decides that he doesn't have time. So make sure he can fit you into his agenda before you mention cash.

So far I've referred to the prospect as someone of the male gender but it could just as well be a female.

Let's get back to the actual interview. The order in which you present your sales pitch, for that's what this interview is, is very important. The points are laid like stepping stones until you come to the final approach, the nitty gritty – hard cash.

In the early part of the interview you explain just how your exercise system works. You pick up a pen and an exercise progress chart and with these you show how you'll make out a schedule to suit his needs and how the exercises will be updated as he makes progress. The pen with which you have made annotations on the exercise chart, is still in your hand as you go into the final approach.

This final approach, though it must appear casual, will be carefully tailored to suit your individual establishment and what you have to offer. You will have covered all the major points mentioned above, hours of opening, length of training sessions, goals etc and then you hear yourself saying, "... and the membership for the year is X dollars ... (you write this down for him to see ...) a slight pause, and then you continue, "... How would you like to pay this ... cash or check?" This last sentence is the most important of the interview. (Note that I am assuming, for simplicity, that your establishment has a simple all-in-one rate for membership. If not, this last approach will have to be modified accordingly.)

Take your potential client to a private area or office to discuss any formalities.

You will notice that we finished with a question, ("How would you like to pay this ... cash or check?") and in doing so we left the ball in the prospect's court. It's a question, which can have several effects. He can say "Cash" or he can say "Check", or even volunteer his credit card. All of these are positive answers – he's joining. Note, we didn't say, "The membership is X dollars ... Would you like to join?" That's because that is a "Yes" or "No" question and it makes it much easier for him to give a negative answer and that's just what you don't want.

Now, you've arrived at the moment of truth, the prospect has all the information and it's up to him. He will usually answer in one of three ways the first, two of which are in your favor. If he says, "Cash," "Check," or mentions his credit card, you start filling in a membership form, perhaps saying something like, "How do you spell that, Mr. Truckendorf?" Start filling in the form even if he has not yet actually pulled out the cash, check book, or credit card. It fills in a void and anyway, you can't say, "Come on let's see the color of your money."

The second type of reaction is, "Have I got to pay this all at once?" This one is easily dealt with. According to your particular price structure, you explain that he can pay so much down and so much a month, or whatever terms you may be offering and again you reach for the membership application.

Number three is not so straightforward. He's the one who says, "I'll have to think about it ..." and usually adds those famous last words, "I'll be back." This one is the most difficult of all, but don't despair. Go through the main points with him again. Get his agreement that his joining would be a good thing and that he would benefit greatly. Then you come back to the point. You ask, "Then what is there to think about?" If you can get him to be truthful, the stumbling block is usually money, though few people like to admit it. You can, diplomatically of course, bring up the matter and offer alternative methods of easy payment; this often does the trick. If it doesn't, you can chalk up another "Beebak"; you can't win 'em all!

Offering alternative methods of payment often convinces the client to sign on the dotted line.

Model: Kim Lyons

I have never worked out what the odds are, but the chances that a Beebak will actually be back are extremely remote, however, sometimes they surprise you!

Before moving on to the next point I'd like to say, to anyone who is already in business, but not yet using an office for the interview – start now and watch your takings increase.

Prospective members, as noted earlier, are very much influenced by what they see and hear on that all-important first visit. One of the things they want to see is people with whom they think they'll feel at home. They want to think they'll fit in. Belonging is very important. Sometimes, when Lady Luck is not on your side, the reverse may happen. Imagine this situation – You are just showing a shy and nervous prospect around on a quiet morning and you have forgotten that the Bedrock Brothers are in there doing their heavy duty monster leg routine. The sight of so much beef, wrestling with so much iron proves devastating and Mr. Quietguy can't get out of the place quick enough. I've lost sales myself through situations like this.

One way you might be able to avoid, or at least minimize this sort of occurrence is to have a heavy section in your workout area. Some sort of alcove or annex where these devoted hard core giants can grunt and groan to their hearts' content – out of sight. I'm not knocking the dedicated beef – trust me boys, but it must be borne in mind that the life-blood of the fitness gym, is a steady influx of people who just want a better than average body. On that all-important first visit, the sight of 52-inch chests and 20-inch arms may not quite create the desired impression.

Puzzle

I'd like to mention here, one of the anomalies of the business. Over the years I have noticed that if someone boldly breezes in with the words, "I've come to join." he'll almost invariably walk out without doing so. Why? To be quite frank, I don't rightly know, but I've formed one or two opinions. It's very difficult to do market research on these things unless you station someone outside your front door to grab and interrogate these escapees.

Why are those four little words, "I've come to join," so often, such bad news? Well, one of my theories is that the prospect came in with the intention of joining, but hadn't actually thought of the economics involved. Hence, when you've shown him the facilities and explained everything and you finally come to your rates, he is put into a state of shock by the mention of serious cash – no matter how good a deal you might be offering. I have discussed this problem with various people in the business, they've noticed this phenomenon too, but nobody has been able to come up with an explanation. Be prepared for this situation. When it happens you'll find yourself asking questions like, "What did I do wrong?" Or thinking that perhaps he didn't like your face or the color of the tiles in the shower room. Not to worry, you'll

Body Works

Progress Chart

Name _____ Schedule _____ Date Started _____

Exercise	S/R	Wt	S/R	Wt	S/R	Wt	S/R	Wt	S/R	Wt	S/R	Wt	S/R	Wt

Instructor _____ Remarks _____

Membership

City Gym

Warning!
Exercise can seriously affect your health

never know. Take heart! Accept that it does happen once in a while and hope that the next inquiry will be more fruitful.

Softly, Softly.

In contrast to the above mentioned character, there is the quiet, hesitant type who comes through the door and explains nervously that he has only come in for some information, actually, he looks as if he's ready to bolt out through the door without warning. Handle him with care, he is one of your best types of prospect and you can do a lot for him.

He probably had a battle mustering up the courage to force himself to come in in the first place. He, more than any other type, needs assurance and reassurance. It may be that he is hoping that improving his physique a little will also change his personality. He's right too; I've seen it happen lots of times. It is amazing how a bit of muscle can increase a person's self-confidence. Assure him that he is making a wise decision in taking up weight training, make him feel at home and let him see that you genuinely want to help him. This type of client usually turns out to be an excellent long-term member.

In passing I'd like to mention that, only once in over forty years experience, did a prospective member tell me that the rates were too high. (I always kept my prices competitive).

This exception was a well-known physique champion, who probably thought we ought to pay him as a box office attraction!

Many overweight people who come along don't like to admit, or even have you mention, the fact that they are overweight. They prefer to say that they "just want to get fit." Okay, go along with it, don't argue. You can put them on weight-reducing schedules all the same, once they've started.

No Universe

There's another type of client that's quite common and fortunately, not too difficult to handle. He is the completely nonathletic, nonmuscular type who says, "I'd like to build up a bit – but I don't want to be a Mr. Universe!" You don't deal with him as I used to many years ago in my youthful arrogance, by saying, "Don't worry my friend, you've got no chance!" No, you go along with him and explain, quite truthfully, that the majority of your members are here for exactly the same reason. They just want better bodies and increased health and fitness. Explain that Mr. Universe aspirants have to put in years of dedicated toil – it's not something that just happens overnight. It's tempting to mention that sometimes, after making good initial gains, people get bitten by the bug and then there's no stopping them. Play this one by ear.

The Guest Pass

Some operators use guest passes. The pass entitles the bearer to a free trial workout and the hope is that having sampled the joys of exercise he will join. However, the passes must be given out on a very selective basis. (After all, it's easy to fill the gym with people who aren't paying.

When giving free trials you must be careful not to let the visitor do too much. Make him too sore and proverbial wild horses won't be able to get him through the door a second time.

Guest passes are particularly useful when a member keeps telling you that he has, "this friend that's very interested ..." Sometimes the offer of a trial session is just what's needed to get him through your portals.

Business Cards

Business cards are a useful tool in the sales armory. You will find that a "beebak" will often ask for one before departing. You must give him one. You never know. Everybody connected with the gym should always have a card or two handy ready to spread the gospel.

Some of the points that I have brought up in this chapter may seem unimportant and others may appear a bit over the top. Let me assure you they are all very important and extremely relevant to the success of your undertaking. The correct psychological approach can make an unimaginable difference in the size of your membership.

The Office

As pointed out in the previous chapter, interviews with prospective members should always take place in an office with both parties seated. I have used the word interview, though perhaps it is not quite the right word. I think consultation would be better because after all, the prospective member is consulting you about his physical condition.

The above statement might seem unremarkable, or even unnecessary, but I have visited many gyms and centres, some of them quite up-market, where enquiries are not dealt with in an office. They are missing out on memberships.

Consider the following situation. Somebody has walked into your reception area and asked for information about the facilities. You offer to show him round and you explain the various equipment to him. You arrive back at the reception area, so far so good. Then you explain the opening times and your membership fees, still standing. He is now in possession of all the facts, he's free to go. The chances are that he'll do just that, perhaps with a cheerful, "Thank you very much, I'll think about it."

Some establishments have a hotel-type, breast-high reception desk. Inquirers are dealt with from behind this barrier. And a barrier it is. From behind such a counter there is little chance of setting up any rapport with the prospect, making him feel at home and wanting to

Never conduct a consultation in your reception area. Take prospective clients back to your office for a private discussion about the facility.

Models: Maurice Murphy and Scott Baur

Your office should be comfortably furnished, but it needn't be extravagantly so. One or two photographs or diplomas on the wall are nice touches.

become a part of the set up. This isn't important in the hotel business, but it is in ours. Again, once he has the information, he's free to go. Oh, it's true that some of these inquirers may come back, but many are lost forever, perhaps to your competitors.

Compare the above with what happens when, after being shown around the installation, your prospective member finds himself seated in the office, in a relaxed atmosphere. He has a chance to get to know you and you have a chance to get to know him, to find out what his aims are, reasons for wanting to join and that sort of thing. It's right here, in this office, that he decides whether or not he is going to join. And it's here that you will be able to give him the assurances that he's probably looking for. Assurance that he would be making a wise decision and assurance that he will get the results he wants.

Now you are in a position to use the sales strategy outlined in the previous chapter. This would be something much more difficult to do standing on the gym floor or at a reception desk.

I had been a gym owner, in London, for about ten years before I discovered what a difference an office could make. A friend of mine came back after a two year stay in America. He had been working in a gym in New York, one of a nationwide chain. He told me how they used these offices, or pitching rooms, as they called them and he convinced me that it was the way to go.

I decided to follow the American lead. There was no separate room available in my gym, so I partitioned off a corner of the gym. I used plywood panels on a wooden frame, cheap and cheerful. From then on all inquirers were led into this den. The results surprised me. By the end of the first week I was amazed to find that my takings had doubled.

The above change proved to be the turning point in my career. This was the early sixties and fitness/bodybuilding was still a long way from becoming the big business that it is today. In fact, up to this point it had always been a struggle to make ends meet. Now, with my increased prosperity, I was over the hump. Within a year I was able to move to a new, larger and much more prestigious premises and I never looked back.

Only one thing bothered me – how many members had I lost before I made this amazing discovery?

GYMBIZ

The office doesn't have to be very large, it doesn't have to take up very much of that precious floor space. If it will house a desk or table and two or three chairs, it will suffice. It is surprising what you can fit into 30 or 40 square feet. The location of the office is important.

Usually just off, or just behind, the reception area is ideal. After showing your prospect round the floor you will normally be heading back in the direction of the reception and also the office. If your office is made by partitioning off a part of the entrance hall or reception area it should be possible to put a hatch or glass panel in one wall so that, even when you are inside you can keep an eye on the comings and goings in reception. This is especially useful in the smaller type of gym where there are not enough staff to keep the reception area permanently manned. You can, if you like make this den open plan style, more of an alcove than an office. This has an advantage. Some people feel that they are being pressurized if they are led into a small office behind a closed door. High pressure selling should be avoided at all costs.

The office, or alcove, should be comfortably furnished, but it needn't be extravagantly so. One or two photographs or diplomas on the wall are nice touches. As the area in question is quite small, we are only talking of five or six square yards, you will be easily able to go to the extravagance of some good quality carpeting. Also, if you can add the luxury of a little pine paneling on the walls, the resulting effect can be quite impressive and cosy too. The photographs should not be of muscular giants, rather of well built athletic-looking people. Remember that some of the people you'll be dealing with have complexes about their physical inadequacies.

It is important that you always keep the office stocked with the tools that you will need in order to make things run smoothly. Membership forms and membership cards, obviously. Equally important, some exercise progress charts and a couple of ballpoint pens. I say a couple of pens, because it's not impossible for one to run dry right on the dotted line.

There are many established operators working without the benefit of an office. To any of these who is wondering why his conversion rate of prospects to members is not as high as it should be, my advice is simple. Start using an office and watch your membership grow.

Your office doesn't have to be very large and it doesn't have to take up very much floor space.

It is important that you always keep the office stocked with the tools that you will need in order to make things run smoothly. Membership forms and membership cards, some exercise progress charts and a couple of ballpoint pens.

Money Savers

There is almost no limit to what can be spent on equipping, furnishing and remodeling, if money is no object. If money is a consideration and you have to keep an eye on the budget, there are a few corners that can be cut.

Floor Covering

This can be an area of major expenditure; it is also an area which poses its own special problems. There are gyms, which are equipped entirely, or almost entirely, with machines. In these emporiums these problems don't exist, or are minimal, because there are no barbells or dumbells or loose discs to crash down on the floor. In these circumstances almost any type of surface will do, tiles, parquet, or carpet. All you need to do is put some rubber pads between the feet of the machines and the floor.

However, most places do have a substantial quota of free weights in addition to machinery and that's when you have to start thinking seriously about the type of floor covering to be used.

A parquet floor is out of the question. It is expensive and it won't stand up to the dropping of weights. A planked wooden floor (floorboards) will splinter. Cement floors, apart from imparting a cold look, will chip and they don't look very pretty. Probably the best solution is carpet. It gives coziness, warmth and even a touch of luxury. You can lay carpet over almost any type of existing flooring. It has the advantage that it will also cover any imperfections, such as hollows left in the wake of a demolished partition wall. Carpet will cushion the effect and dampen the sound, of falling iron. It's amazing how some people just toss the plates on the floor when changing weights.

It isn't necessary to buy expensive carpet because the weights will cut it anyway, whatever the quality. Buy at the cheaper end of the market and be prepared to renew it every three or four years. If you have to replace it any earlier, it means you are getting very heavy traffic. If business is that good, you won't mind forking out for a new carpet.

Keep a watchful eye on your flooring. Making repairs right away will make your floors last longer.

Photo courtesy Gold's Gym, Venice, CA

You can prolong the life of your carpet by placing strips of rubber or plastic stair matting in any heavy traffic areas. This is particularly important in front of barbell and dumbell racks and other places where weights are habitually put down on the floor, between exercises. Rubber matting comes in various colors. Plastic has an advantage worth noting in that it is also available in transparent form. This of course means that it will blend in well with any color scheme that you may have. Whichever matting you choose, having it well placed can double the life of your carpet.

Between the carpet and the floor you should put underlay. This increases the cushioning effect of the carpet above and gives the illusion that the carpet itself is of better quality. This is a one-time expense, as the underlay will last a lifetime. It's the carpet that takes all the cuts and bruises and therefore needs periodic renewal.

You can delay carpet renewal by keeping a watchful eye on things. Look out for small cuts and punctures. Deal with them as soon as you spot them. They can usually be stuck down with contact adhesive. If not dealt with right away a tiny cut soon becomes a big rip.

There are plates on the market, that are sheathed in a shock absorbing vinyl material.

Nothing looks worse than beautifully designed equipment with tattered upholstery.

Photo courtesy Gold's Gym, Venice, CA

These of course cause less damage to floors, but the initial outlay may be somewhat higher.

Fiberboard or hardboard, which comes in handy 8 x 4 sheets, makes a hardwearing and inexpensive floor covering. The only drawback is that it's not pretty, however, it has its merit. I used it in one gym where we had a heavy training area, reserved for the hardcore bodybuilders and powerlifters. We laid it face down, that is to say, with the wrong side up. The pattern on this surface offers a nonslip grip. It was given two or three coats of green paint and was as good as new after ten years service.

This material expands when damp, so it is a good idea to wet the sheets and leave them lying flat overnight to dry, before laying and securing in their final positions. If this precaution is not taken they may expand when painted. The result will be an undulating floor.

Sheets of plywood can also be used as floor covering. Like hardboard it comes in 8 x 4 sheets and is easy to handle and lay. It can be varnished and gives a better appearance than hardboard. While not suitable for a main gym floor, I have seen this material used as flooring for an aerobics studio and the effect was quite pleasing.

Upholstery

One of the recurring costs of running a gym is the replacement of upholstery on benches, machines and other equipment. Nothing looks worse than a gleaming, beautifully designed machine with tattered upholstery. Most of this unnecessary wear and tear is caused by thoughtlessness on the part of the members, many of whom put weights down directly on the upholstery, often not too gently. Though instructors can, and do, point out these little errors, they can't be constantly hounding the members. You can however put up small notices in strategic positions. This will help discourage Jack the Ripper and save you money.

While on the subject of notices, I am reminded of one that I saw in a busy, but tidy gym – "Put it right back in the rack Jack." This of course was aimed at that other menace, the guy that always leaves his weights lying around after use.

Fabrication

Barbell and dumbell racks and also benches present another area where money can often be saved. It may be worthwhile to have them fabricated to your own specifications rather than buy them from a manufacturer. Your local welding, or light engineering firm, would probably be pleased to do the job. For benches, racks and stands square section steel tube of 50 mm (2 inches) will serve you well, though for extra heavy duty you can go up to 75 mm or more. You may want to tackle the manufacture of some more ambitious pieces of equipment in this manner. Your fabricator will want some sort of a rough drawing to work from, but this should not be too difficult with all the magazine and catalog photographs available.

Your personal computer can be used to produce membership application forms, membership cards, exercise schedule cards and stationary at negligible expense. Eat your heart out Mr. Printer! If colored card is used on some of the above, you can get some pleasing results.

Your internal signs, such as "No Smoking," "Ladies Only" and "Wipe your feet," once the domain of the sign writer, can now all be turned out on the computer – and in next to no time.

A personal computer can save you lots of money as it can be used to produce virtually all your printed matter. Also, if you load the right software you can use it to control the comings and goings of your members and receive prior warning of when they are due to pay. There is one system available which includes a turnstile which is hooked up with your PC. If someone's card has expired, it won't let him in. Such a system costs money and I think the expense is only really justified if you're running a pretty big and busy operation.

Another field where you can save money is on the printing of nice glossy brochures showing the inside of your gym or leisure centre. My advice to anybody just starting out in the business is very simple. Don't have any printed. Save your money instead. They can be very expensive, if you want a good job done and perhaps surprisingly, they rarely bring in enough revenue to pay for themselves. There is more about this in Chapter 14 (Advertising and Publicity).

Perhaps the biggest savings of all can be made in the purchase of the actual gym equipment; the very nuts and bolts of the industry. As stated elsewhere, professional gym equipment and weights are so intrinsically rugged that they last a lifetime. As far

It may be worthwhile to have racks fabricated to your own specifications rather than buy them from a manufacturer.

Photo courtesy Gold's Gym, Venice, CA

as weights are concerned, this makes a very strong case for not buying new, especially if you have the time to look around.

All over the world there are periodicals that specialize in classified ads. The main ones in America are Loot and Recycler and their pages have long been a source of second hand weights and equipment to legions of physical culturists. The amount of second-hand gear on the market is not surprising when you think of the thousands of people who buy weights year in year out, with the intention of training at home. Many, perhaps most of them, fall by the wayside. Lots of them just drop out forever, training solo is tough. The rest do the sensible thing, they join a gym. The result is pretty much the same either way – a neglected barbell gathering dust under the bed. This constant supply of cast iron is always available and by studying the ads in the columns of the above-mentioned papers, you'll soon get an idea of the going rate per pound. These "Looting Recyclers" and their readers love to haggle and in fact, it is rumored that they invented the word. They definitely invented some quaint abbreviations, including W.H.Y. and O.N.O. (what have you and or near offer). It's essential to master this bartering jargon in order to use the papers to your best advantage. You also need G.S.O.H. (good sense of humor).

Photo courtesy Gold's Gym, Venice, CA

It may mean a little travelling to pick up the stuff and in some cases, a little work afterwards to rejuvenate it. A coat of Hammerite works wonders in this direction. This crackle finish paint has the advantage that you can apply it straight over rust without any special preparation.

You can find lots of good used equipment in the newspaper and recycling periodicals.

It is also very quick drying, which means that you can always retouch any chips or blemishes without having the apparatus, or weights, out of action all day.

Also in these periodicals you may find all sorts of other goodies like mirrors and dressing room benches. Sometimes you may come across ads for small firms who offer gym equipment. Their advertisements are well worth following up. They are usually small, or one man, businesses working out of small lock-up workshops. With their low overhead they are able to produce equipment at much lower prices than the big name manufacturers.

You may find that their products may not be as spectacular in appearance as the more expensive ones but often the construction is more rugged. The man running such a business is usually someone who has had gym experience himself. He understands your needs and very often will modify his designs to meet your personal requirements. This might be useful if you have come up with some special idea for a new piece of equipment. It's also something that the big boys might be reluctant to do. For a substantial order the small man is also more likely to be persuaded to give a handsome discount.

When choosing equipment it certainly pays to look around and consider the various options. In this department the best buys do not always come from the pages of a glossy catalog.

Price Structure

Membership fees and method of payment vary greatly, not only from one gym to another, but also from town to town and region to region. Just how you structure your membership fees will be dependent to a large extent on what neighboring establishments are charging. That is, unless you are in a zone where there is no competition at all – an enviable, but rare position these days.

There are various alternatives open and the main ones are listed here for comparison.

• Yearly All-Inclusive Membership
Members pay an all-inclusive fee for the year. Members can attend as often as they like, using the weight-training and fitness facilities and the sauna, if available. Aerobics, Martial arts and any other class activities, are usually charged separately, unless this is the member's main interest, in which case the activity is included in lieu of weight-training.

• Half Yearly or Quarterly Membership
Usually offered as an alternative to yearly membership, but does not work out as economical for the member.

• Monthly Subscription
A set amount is charged every month, per activity. An extra joining fee, may or may not be charged. If charged, this is usually the same as the monthly rate.

• Session Fee (daily)
This is simply pay as you go, on a use it – don't use it basis.

Of the four methods, looked at from a business point of view, the yearly membership is the best. The member has paid for the year up front, it's up to him to use the facilities provided. If he drops out, he loses out. Some people like the idea of paying in advance, it gives them an incentive to keep at it. They argue that if they have paid for it they are going to make sure that they get what they've paid for. In practice they often drop out just the same.

Members can pay an all-inclusive fee for the year which allows them to attend as often as they like, using the weight-training and fitness facilities and the sauna, if available. Photo courtesy of Gold's Gym, Venice, CA

44

Mike O'Hearn

Gyms and leisure centres that charge on a yearly basis are usually able to quote a yearly figure that is much lower than their competitors who offer similar facilities on a monthly basis. However, whether or not you are able to command a yearly subscription, depends very much on the quality and location of your establishment. Ideally, you will be situated in a thriving city, or if not, in a high-income area. Your installation and presentation must be right up to scratch.

Centers that have a yearly membership system usually offer half-yearly or quarterly rates as alternatives. Neither of these will work out as economically, to the client, as the full year. If they did, then the yearly membership would be much harder to sell.

The monthly rate system is probably in use in more gyms worldwide than any other. With its lower initial outlay, even if a joining fee is charged, it is within easier reach of those on a budget. This means that it is much easier to sell than the yearly system.

Many gyms that charge a joining fee in addition to the first month, also stipulate that if the member drops out for say, three or four months, he must rejoin if he wants to start again. If you are thinking of going for monthly payments, whether or not you can ask for a joining fee in addition, will depend very much on what the competition in your area is doing.

If you decide on a monthly payment system, you have the option of two methods of collection.

1. All subscriptions due on the first of the month.

2. Subscription due one month from joining date. This means that if a member joins on say, the tenth of the month he will be due to pay again on the tenth of the following month. In this way members are free to join at any time during the month and not just at the beginning.

Of the two methods, the second makes for better, and more evenly spread cash flow and increased takings. The latter is true because the prospective member doesn't have to wait till the first of next month to start; he can join today, whatever the date. Why be ruled by the calendar?

Session fees make for a lower monthly gross. They gym operator is completely at the mercy of his members and their whims. If it rains they don't come. If there's football on TV they don't come, or if they just feel a bit lazy they don't come. Missing a session that has not been paid for is painless, for the client at least. The more sessions missed the easier it becomes to give the whole thing a miss and drop out for good.

Sad to say, the gross takings from such as operation, more often than not, aren't really sufficient to support even an average installation, unless the overhead is unusually low.

It is true that there are various leisure and sports centres, run by local authorities, which work on a session basis. This is fine for them because they aren't really interested in showing a profit and they are not really in the market place. In many cases this is just as well, as they wouldn't survive.

If one of these municipal centres exists in your area, I don't think there is any need to view it as competition. Rarely do they provide the standard of service that a privately owned place can offer. That personal touch, which is the hallmark of the privately run gym, is just not there. Private enterprise, like Avis, has to try that little bit harder and the members benefit. Sometimes they do have good staff and competent instructors in these institutions but the aims and ambitions of these instructors may differ widely from those in the private or commercial sector. An instructor may tend to devote more time to an up and coming local athlete while a beginner doesn't get the encouragement he needs. A similar situation exists in some schools, where the teachers favor the more brilliant pupils at the expense of the less fortunate kids.

When calculating price structure we have to remember that a high dropout rate is part of the business. Time after time one finds that members drop out even though they may have paid in advance. Many times when checking the books, I have found that some who had paid for a year's membership had not lasted 3 months. They just disappear leaving nine months' training going to waste. Someone pointed out to me that it was a bit like the mustard industry, they make a larger part of their profit, not out of mustard consumed, but out of that which is left on the plate.

Now at first sight the above might give the impression that we're pulling something of a fast one here, charging people for something that they haven't had, but in fact, those who don't use up all their membership time are subsidizing those who do.

Just think of what would happen if every member who paid for a year's membership in advance, actually attended for a whole year. Or, if every monthly member who had paid a joining fee, kept coming, month after month. The result is quite predictable. Take an average sized gym signing on say, five or six new people each week. It would be full to overflowing long before the year was out. Membership would have to be closed. One alternative would be

Photo courtesy of Gold's Gym, Venice, CA

to increase the membership charges and have fewer people, each paying more money. Fortunately, at least for the stalwarts who don't drop out, we don't have to resort to this alternative and those who fall by the wayside continue to subsidize those who don't.

Reviewing the alternatives, I would say again that your choice of price structure would depend very much on the location and the standard of your operation.

Obviously, if your geographical location is right and your installation is up to the mark, you would be well advised to opt for the yearly membership method. There is no doubt that this is where the most money is.

On the other hand, if your set-up is of a more modest nature, or if you're not quite in the right area, you may have to go for the monthly system. Of course it may be that you have strong competition in your chosen area and then your strategy will have to be tailored accordingly.

Photo courtesy of Gold's Gym, Venice, CA

If you decide on the monthly system I think it would be a mistake not to charge a joining fee. This could be anything from the equivalent of one to three month's subscription. Bear in mind that if your joining fee is only the equivalent of one month's subscription and if you enroll 20 new members each month, their enrollment fees add up to the equivalent of another 20 who don't take up any floor space. It's a source of revenue that you can't afford to overlook. It might even pay the rent. By the way, 20 new members a month is by no means an over optimistic figure. It's less than one a day and you should be able to do better than that.

Finally we come to payment on a session basis. My advice is, unless there are in your case, very unusual mitigating circumstances – don't do it. By mitigating circumstances I mean something like first class premises, rent-free (or almost) and in a prime position.

Ultimately the choice is yours and you will have to decide which method suits your particular case best, though the choice really lies between yearly and monthly membership. Of the two, monthly is the easier to sell because you will be asking for a smaller lump sum. Alternatively, if you are going for the yearly method, more salesmanship is required because you'll be talking about serious money. However as stated above with the right set-up in the right location, there is great commercial scope in this approach and the content of chapters 6 and 7 will be of the greatest importance.

Whatever method you choose, be positive and businesslike about it and you'll be well on the road to success.

Partners, or Go It Alone?

Many businesses are born as the brainchild of two friends and this is quite understandable. Good friends often have similar ideas and a similar outlook. They decide to go into business as partners.

In the gym business they are usually partners before they go into business – training partners. Friends that know each other well through exercising together, often for a number of years. They confide in each other that they have long been thinking of going into the business and so the idea begins to take shape.

It can't be denied that having a partner makes good economic sense. Any business requires an initial capital outlay. By taking a half-share partner, you immediately split this outlay down the middle, thereby reducing the amount of capital that you, personally, have at stake. You will also, of course, have to share your profits with him.

This last point brings us to the first question. Is the operation you have in mind big enough to support both of you? If the answer is "no" or even "don't know," you are on shaky ground before you start. You'll have to go it alone, or rethink and plan something bigger.

One point in favor of partnerships is that nowadays it is very difficult to run a one-person gym and even if you have only a moderate membership you will find that you need to take on paid help. With a partner of course, you can split the workload and thus perhaps, stave off the day when you have to take on extra help. Though if things go well you're going to need more staff, sooner or later. Still, the sharing of responsibility makes life a lot easier.

How well do you really know your proposed partner? This is the question that both parties concerned should be asking themselves. He is as honest as the day is long (otherwise he wouldn't be a friend of yours) and despite all those old jokes about one partner finding the other with his hand in the cash box, you just know he could never do anything like that. It is also a sad fact that many lifelong friends fall out once they go into business together.

Having a partner makes good economic sense, but think long and hard before choosing one.
– Lee Apperson and Debbie Kruck

Obviously then, anyone should think hard and long before embarking on a partnership. It's a bit like getting married except that nowadays in the case of husband and wife, divorce may be a little easier. I can think of several Dynamic Duos who have made it in the gym business. Then again, I also know some long-time friends who have split up over the gym business.

When the two partners have personal attributes that compliment each other, the results can be very positive. For example if one partner is good on the administrative and publicity side of things and the other is a born teacher, things can work out very well. Sometimes one is a business genius and the other is more artistic and creative. Opposites do not only attract, in many cases each party may be the catalyst that the other needs.

One partnership that I know of, which worked like the proverbial house on fire, was between two friends from entirely different backgrounds. One had previously worked in an accountant's office and the other was a carpenter. Their paths had crossed when they started training at the same gym.

When they decided to go into business together they found that the blending of their academic and practical skills worked out perfectly to their mutual benefit.

Partnerships can also work well when the partners come from two different disciplines, such as weight training and karate. In these cases each runs his side of the business. One advantage of this is that each is able to encourage his pupils to participate in the other activity. The result is more business for both.

Silent Partner

There are businesses where a silent partner is involved. The partner has put his money into the business, but nothing else. He doesn't share any of the workload and is only interested in what he takes out. To him it's just another investment and the other partner has to do all the work. My advise is, steer clear of this situation. Don't take on a silent partner just as a means of raising capital, he's got to bring something more than mere money into the business. There are other ways of raising cash without having a silent partner on your back forever.

Couples

There are of course, many husband and wife partnerships in the business and these work very well. Each member of the team deals with his or her own sex. If one of the pair has training in another discipline, such as aerobics or martial arts, this can be a definite advantage. Couples have another advantage over ordinary partnerships, in that they only have one household to support. Therefore they don't need quite the same income.

If you are considering partnership you must draw up and sign a contract. You may think this is not necessary, you may say, "Hell, we've known each other for fifteen years, who needs a contract. We've got each other's word, haven't we?" That's just why you need a contract – because you are great friends and because you've known each other fifteen years!

Alternatively you can form a registered company in which you are joint shareholders. This is usually done on a fifty-one to forty-nine basis; this gives one of you what is known as the controlling share. Which one? Well, you'll have to ponder on this weighty subject, all I can say is, "It's up to you – you know the guy!" What's that – he's reading this too?

Partnership, or company, you will need to take legal advice before proceeding. In either case, such joining of forces should not be undertaken on a rush decision. Both parties should do their homework thoroughly before tying the knot.

On the Gym Floor

What happens on the gym floor is really the end product of all the planning and thinking that goes into the opening of any gym or health studio. It is where the action is and on this action depends the success of the whole operation. It is the place where members and staff really get to know each other. Also, it's the place where the members become acquainted with each other. And it's where they form and often air, their opinions of the gym and its management.

What the members see and hear on the gym floor is what will really form their image of your gym. One of the most important factors to consider is the matter of dress.

Dress

As discussed in Chapter 5, a professional approach must be adopted throughout your operation and nowhere is this more important than in the exercise area. Naturally, anybody on the gym floor, giving instruction, will be suitably dressed. All members must wear appropriate training gear too, right down to rubber soled shoes. It is necessary to be very firm on this point. I have seen people turn up on the training floor in a variety of garbs, ranging from tight fitting jeans to Y-front underwear. Neither of these is in line with the desired professional image. Imagine the effect it could have on a prospective member being shown round for the first time.

Visitors

Visitors and spectators must not be allowed in the exercise area. Sometimes it requires a little diplomacy to achieve this, but you must insist on it. Usually the would-be offender is a young man who has brought his girlfriend along to

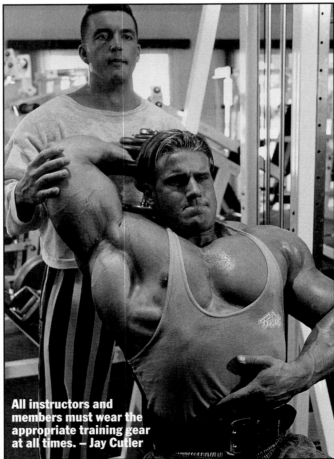

All instructors and members must wear the appropriate training gear at all times. – Jay Cutler

watch him train. You can normally get round this one by pointing out that only people in training gear are allowed on the floor. If your layout permits it you may be able to arrange some seating with a view of the gym floor. I actually had a gym with visitors' gallery.

Encouragement

Members should have their own personal exercise schedule cards. These should be kept in a filing box, in an easily accessible place. Instructors should check from time to time to see that progress is being made. That is to say that the weight used, or the number of repetitions done, is being increased as progress is made. It gives the member an opportunity to see that we are really interested in him. It also gives the instructor a chance to drop in a few words of encouragement. Encouragement is a key factor if you are after increased member retention and a lower drop-out rate. Many of the more advanced people won't want this kind of help, preferring to plan their own routines and monitor their own progress.

Don't wait till the machine becomes unusable, take care of the problem right away.

Model: Alonzo Vasquez

With these advanced people, the time to help is when they are performing an exercise that requires heavy weight, such as bench presses or squats. The instructor can step in and do a little spotting. He can also give a word of encouragement during those last two reps. Encouragement and inspiration are what the instructor's job is all about, these things are every bit as important as the instructing itself.

Breakdown

Occasionally, something in the gym will break down; usually it's one of the machines. There is just one inflexible rule about this – get it fixed as soon as humanly possible. If possible you should try to get the machine back in service the same day. Should this not be possible, promise the members that it will be fixed by the next day, and make sure that it is.

Some members get very attached to certain pieces of apparatus and often they will tell you that your leg press, or your pec-dek, is the best they've ever used or seen. Sometimes this is the sole reason why they prefer your gym to another. Should they suddenly be deprived of the use of their favorite piece of hardware, they may become very dissatisfied. You have an obligation to your members. They have paid their membership fees and you've got to see that everything is kept running smoothly.

Maintenance

You can avoid the type of problem mentioned above by regular maintenance. Most exercise machines rely on the use of steel cables and these must be periodically checked for wear. One by one the fine strands break, causing jags. Once you see that a cable has more than a couple of these whiskers it's time to renew it. Don't wait till it becomes unusable, or worse still, breaks.

Remember, that it isn't always necessary to go back to the manufacturers to get replacement cables. Boat supply shops and hardware stores stock suitable cable in all sizes.

If properly looked after, your equipment should last a lifetime.

Model: Alonzo Vasquez

Ball races in pulleys and other moving parts should be inspected and if necessary greased periodically. Properly looked after, these should last a lifetime.

Types of members

Gym membership can be broken down into three groups:

A – Beginners

These are people who have recently started and have three months or less experience. Nobody can forecast whether or not they will move on to the next group. Many, alas, will drop out forever. Some not even lasting three months. You can reduce the fall-out by giving these people more attention.

B – Intermediate

They have made it through the novice period but it is impossible to say whether or not they will become true converts to the faith. Again much depends on the way they are treated and the service they get.

C – Dedicated

These members are committed to the physical culture lifestyle one hundred percent. They will continue exercising for years to come, summer and winter, rain or shine. If they disappear from your gym they will turn up in another. Look after them and they'll stay.

Each of these three groups has to be treated in a different way, if you want to keep them all happy and keep your membership flourishing at the same time.

The beginners in group A have to be given lots of attention, they have to be kept interested and above all, they have to make gains. They have to see that it's working and that the effort is worthwhile.

Any experienced instructor or gym operator knows that whatever you do, even if you spoon-feed them with high protein on the gym floor, a high percentage of today's beginners will not be there in three months time. It's one of the facts of gym life, but it's no excuse for not trying as hard as you can to reduce this drop out rate.

The intermediates in Group B also need lots of encouragement. Some of them are going to become life converts and it's up to you to make sure that the number is as high as possible. They have already made some initial gains, in health, fitness and visible muscle and they know the value of what they are doing. You've got to get them to keep at it.

In weight training, progress is never steady. The bodybuilder, from time to time reaches so called sticking points. He doesn't seem to be making any further progress, enthusiasm ebbs. He may even get a feeling he is going backwards. This is peak drop out time. A good instructor will sense this and do all he can to put it right. Often the cure is a complete change of training routine, or, heaven forbid, a week's complete lay-off.

Pretty much the same applies to the "slimmers." They too reach plateaus and the instructor should be able to help them over the hump. Again a change in routine will often make all the difference.

With their good physiques and obvious strength and fitness, experienced bodybuilders are an inspiration to the less experienced members. – Enzo Ferrari and Tho-mass Benagli

Now Group C, the dyed-in-the-wool barbell addicts. Asking them to miss a workout would be like suggesting that they take castor oil. There is no danger of them dropping out either. What can we do for them? In many cases we can't teach them a lot. Some of them have been at it for years. They have great value, not only as members, but for their box office value too. We need them. With their good physiques and obvious strength and fitness, they are an inspiration to the less experienced members. They are in fact the "After" part of a living "Before 'n' After" ad for the gym. Often they assist by giving advice and encouragement to newer members.

These die-hards are hooked on iron. As I said above, if they leave your gym it will only be to move to another. You have to make sure that they don't leave. They have to be made to feel at home, that this is where they belong. You have to listen to them too. If they want an extra piece of equipment or a special kind of bar, if within reason let them have it. You don't want them to go to Big Jim's Gym just because he's got a preacher bench and you haven't.

There is another point that no gym owner can afford to overlook. It is from this group that he will probably choose his next instructor, should he need one.

Rules

Each member, on joining, will have signed a form saying that he will abide by the rules of the house. While nobody likes rules and regimentation, some norms must be preserved. The rules should be prominently displayed on the gym floor and in addition it is a good idea to put extra notices in strategic spots where, otherwise, transgressions might occur. Below is a suggested list of some of the most important.

• All weights to be replaced after use.

This is probably the most important rule of all, if you don't want the gym floor to look like a battlefield.

• No weights to be placed on benches or upholstery.

It never ceases to amaze me how little regard some people have for soft furnishings. Nothing looks tattier than Naugahyde when it's torn, ripped or scuffed.

• No feet on the upholstery.

This is to discourage people who think it's good to bench press with your feet up on the bench instead of firmly on the floor.

• No training without T-shirt or vest.

This keeps the benches and equipment sweat-free.

• No horseplay.

Goes without saying.

All weights should be replaced after use.

• No drinks (orange juice, protein, etc.) to be consumed on the gym floor.

The cause of horrible stains, often, in the case of carpet, irremovable. All drinking restricted to the juice bar area.

• No equipment to be used for other than its intended purpose.

To discourage those who want to improvise, balancing benches on top of each other and other dangerous practices.

• No glasses or glass bottles in shower area.

Plastic bottles only, means there will be no cut feet.

• Don't monopolize equipment.

Equipment should be shared with others who might want to use it during rest periods. Normally three people can comfortably alternate on the same bar or machine.

Quite a forbidding list and it seems to be loaded with "No-no's," but if you make sure that everyone abides by these rules, word will soon get around that yours is a serious and well run establishment. You will attract serious and well-run people. Neglect of this side of things can turn a super, well-equipped operation into shambles in no time at all.

Safety

It is the obligation of the management to take out insurance covering the members against accident and/or injury in the gym. In a situation where only weight training and fitness exercises are practiced, injury is very rare indeed, but nevertheless, certain precautionary measures must be taken.

• Collars on all fixed barbells and dumbells should be frequently checked. Preferably they should be of the Allen screw type. The key or wrench should be held by the management to avoid people tampering with the fixed poundages.

• Members doing heavy bench pressing or squatting should have a spotter standing by. Plates should be locked on with outer collars. These can be of the quick-release type.

• Skipping and skipping ropes should be banned in the weight training area.

• Nobody should be allowed to train in bare feet.

• Make sure that your weight-training area has sufficient elbow room and that people using the various benches are not crowded together. Free weights need a little free space.

Despite the heavy metal that is hoisted, and the machinery that is used in weight training, the risk of injury is almost nil. In over forty years as a gym owner I never saw anybody suffer anything worse than a cut finger. In aerobics there is the occasional ligament problem and that's about all.

Martial arts, of course, by their very nature, present a somewhat different story. Here it's up to the instructor to see that everything is done properly in order to minimize risk of injury. In the hands of a good instructor there is no real risk until the students reach the "free fighting" stage. On no account must anybody be supervising such activity unless he is fully qualified.

Warming Up

In all sports and physical activities there is a risk of soft tissue injury if the body is not prepared by suitable warm-up exercises. Make sure that everybody does warmup before starting a session.

In the heavier weight training exercises, such as bench presses, presses and squats, it's a good idea to make sure that pupils do a couple of light break-in sets before they do the real working movements.

Now, while the above advice is only common sense, not everybody heeds it. Try to make sure that everyone knows about the importance of warming up. Anyone who ignores the advice cannot blame the instructor or management for any consequent injury.

You'll find one in every gym.

In every gym there's at least one bright spark who insists on doing special exercises, usually of his own invention. Now, if these movements are simply silly and ineffective, they can do little harm. Perhaps the only damage caused will be to your reputation, if a visitor from

For common sense reasons, no one should be allowed to train barefoot.

Model: Tito Raymond

another gym happens to be watching. The real problem is that very often, some of these silly movements are downright dangerous. In these cases they must be discouraged at once.

You may show the offender a more conventional alternative which will achieve the desired effect. You can also point out, diplomatically, that really there has been very little new in the way of weight training exercises in the last thirty or forty years. This is true, any movements that were any good were invented long ago. It is only the manner of application that has changed as our knowledge has increased.

Beginners' Weight Training Schedule

Month after month and year after year, the muscle magazines publish exercise schedules. In fact, training articles are the staple food of the physical culture press. However, most of these articles are about champion bodybuilders and their training routines and as the glossy photographs show, these schedules can be fairly complicated. The main concern of the gym operator or instructor is to provide simple, uncomplicated routines for beginners and members of limited experience. He must give advice and guidance to the more advanced, but by and large it will be found that these members more or less take care of themselves.

There are dozens of different weight training exercises in popular use but most of these are really variations on a very small number of basic movements. Nevertheless, the permutations in exercise routines are endless and far beyond the scope of a book of this size. I am sure that anyone aspiring to a career in health and fitness, is already well equipped to write training schedules. However, I feel that when dealing with beginners one should largely stick to the basics, saving the variations for later schedules. I have laid out some typical beginners' routines, which may be used as guidelines.

Beginners can be divided into two main categories, those that want to lose weight and those who don't. In either case there is a desire for an increased level of general fitness, but this is often, at this stage, a secondary consideration. These two groups can be subdivided again into men and women.

Frank Sepe

Let's take the ladies first. I think it's fair to say that the majority of women first go to the gym because of a weight problem. Usually the problem areas are the waist, hips and thighs. It is natural therefore that for these ladies, the schedule prescribed will be designed mainly to hit those areas. General work for the rest of the body will also be given. This will help with weight reduction by virtue of the fact that all exercise burns calories. As in all cases this schedule will be performed after some light, freehand warm-up exercises. This is followed by a session on the stationary bicycle. On the first day, two or three minutes at a reasonably brisk pace, will suffice. In consequent sessions this time can be increased considerably. The stationary bike is a great calorie burner and it is a first class cardiovascular exercise machine.

These ladies never welcome the mention of the dreaded word "calories," but nevertheless we've got to persuade them to adjust their food intake a little. A high protein, low carbohydrate diet, combined with a suitable exercise program will work wonders. I have noticed that the word "diet" is not very popular either. As a result it has become more politically correct to talk of "watching one's food intake," rather than "going on a diet."

Penny Price

Below is a typical reducing schedule for a woman whose main problem areas are hips, thighs and waist.
1. Trunk twisting
2. Leg raises
3. Abdominal crunches
4. Free squats
5. Thigh Adductor machine
6. Overhead pulley (Lat machine)
7. Dumbell flyes
8. Knee-over (floor exercise)

The above exercises should all be done for three sets of twenty repetitions. However, for a complete beginner, three full sets should not be attempted on any exercise on the first day. One set, or two at the most, will suffice if she is to avoid too much unnecessary stiffness and suffering.

Also, on the first day, a full twenty reps may not be possible on many of the exercises, don't insist. The beginner should do as many as is possible without fighting too hard. The required number of reps can be built up over a period of several workouts. It may take two or three weeks to reach the prescribed number. It's better to progress slowly than to push the beginner too hard. The resulting discomfort could put her off exercise permanently.

In the exercises where weights are used, style is more important than actual weight at this stage. When an increase in weight, or resistance is made, make sure that it is not at the expense of style.

The above schedule should be followed three to four times weekly, for a period of eight or twelve weeks. At the end of this period results should be assessed and the pupil should be put on a new routine.

Now let's look at a program for a young lady who hasn't a weight problem but she feels she'd like to fill out her frame a little with some curves in the right places.

First there is a warm-up period and this is exactly as in the schedule above, some free-hand movements and then a stint on the bicycle. She is now ready for the first exercise.

1. Situps
2. Barbell curls
3. Triceps extensions
4. Bench presses
5. Dumbell lateral raises
6. Overhead pulley (Lat machine)
7. Squat with bar
8. Sidebends

Start

Melissa Lutzenburger performs squats with strict form.

Finish

Training sessions should be three times a week and the above exercises should all be performed for three sets of ten repetitions. Though on the first day, to avoid undue stiffness a maximum of two sets will be enough. In some cases it is wise to only let the member do one set. This is something that has to be judged by the instructor on the spot and of course, applies to all beginners.

The weights used at the beginning should be well within the pupil's capability. This poundage can be gradually increased over the weeks, but never pushed too much and always make sure that all movements are performed in good style.

This course should be followed three times weekly for eight to twelve weeks. Explain to your pupil that this is basically a muscle-toning course and as muscles respond to exercise when rested, it is best to work out on alternate days, leaving rest days in between. For example, Monday, Wednesday and Friday (always the most popular) or Tuesday, Thursday and Saturday.

Encourage a good wholesome diet with plenty of protein.

At the end of the allotted time on this schedule progress will be checked, results noted and encouragement given. The routine will be changed and perhaps extra work given for areas that are not up to par.

Now we shall look at the male beginners, taking the "slimmers" first. The male fat-haven is the waistline. He doesn't have the hip and thigh problem that the women have, the fat just collects in one place – the gut. As with the ladies he has to be gently lectured on what to eat and what not to eat and put on a calorie-burning routine. Below is a typical schedule.

Start with a short period of free-hand warm-up movement followed by three to five minutes on the stationary bicycle (this time should be increased once the initial stiffness period has passed). After this, go to the first exercise.

1. Leg raises
2. Situps
3. Squats
4. Side bends
5. Bench presses
6. Curls
7. Bent-over rows
8. Upright rows

This schedule is to be followed up to four times a week for eight to twelve weeks. Trunk and waist exercises three sets of twenty. Other movements three sets of twelve to fifteen reps. Weights are gradually increased as strength builds up. Again, as in all weight training, see that the pupil doesn't sacrifice style for poundage. Reassessment will be made at the end of the course and the next program planned accordingly.

Be sure not to sacrifice style for poundage.
– Joe Spinello

GYMBIZ

Now we come to the normal healthy young man who simply wants to improve his body. He wants to pack on some muscle and build up in general. He is really the easiest of all clients to deal with. While it's true that he will still need lots of encouragement from time to time, at least you won't have to tell him to curtail his food intake, as I said earlier, this never makes you popular.

He needs plenty of good food and his diet should have a high protein content. He can also make good use of various body-building food supplements now on the market. He should train only three times per week during this initial period, though very often he may want to do more. His enthusiasm must be curbed and you must point out that the muscles only grow on the rest days. This program should be adhered to strictly for twelve weeks. After a warm-up, as in the previous schedule, start as follows:

1. Situps
2. Upright rows
3. Squats
4. Barbell curls
5. Triceps extensions
6. Bench presses
7. Overhead pulley or chinning bar
8. Calf machine

In order to build a muscle, it is necessary to constantly increase the demands that you put on it.
– Jason Arntz

The leg exercises in the above schedule will be performed for three sets of twenty. The legs, particularly the calves, can take, and need a lot of work. In the other movements three sets of ten will suffice. As with other types of beginners, your aspiring bodybuilder must be broken in gently. With only one or two sets on the first day. On the squat my recommendation is to start off with only one set. Only increase this when the initial soreness has worn off. In the case of the thighs, this can take a few days.

In order to build a muscle it is necessary to constantly increase the demands that you make on it. For this reason it is essential to increase the weight or resistance used, gradually. The bodybuilder must be encouraged to do so but as stressed elsewhere, never at the expense of style.

It is important to have wall charts showing all the major exercises, so that members can consult them if ever in doubt and the instructor is otherwise occupied.
– Mike O'Hearn

After finishing this course, the pupil and the teacher will be pleased to note substantial gains in both strength and muscle. Now is the time to move on to slightly more advanced training methods. In the following three months extra sets can be added for those bodyparts which may be lagging behind in progress. However, training days should be kept down to three a week, on alternate days, until the novice has at least six months training under his belt. During this embryo period it's easy to make progress. Later when progress has become stuck, or has slowed down, you can introduce things like the split training system.

The split system divides the muscles into two groups and these are worked on alternate days. This means that one group, say legs and back, are resting on the day that the other group, for example, chest, arms and shoulders, are working. On a system like this it's possible to train four to six times a week. This sort of routine is definitely not for beginners and should not be attempted by anybody with less than six months solid experience.

It will be noted that the above schedules are mainly based on the use of free weights. This is mainly in the interest of clarity. In cases where it is desirable or convenient, machines may be substituted for barbells and dumbells.

The instructor will, as a matter of course, take any pupil right through a new routine to make sure that he knows exactly how to perform each exercise. However it is important to have wall charts showing all the major exercises, so that members can consult them if ever in doubt and the instructor is otherwise occupied.

Personal Trainer

The explosion that created the health and fitness industry in recent years, also created one or two interesting spin-offs. One of these is a whole new profession, that of personal trainer. Usually, these personal trainers visit their clients to give them exercise in their own homes, but occasionally they accompany them when training in a gym.

The men and women who make up this band of personal trainers are, like everybody else in the industry, enthusiasts themselves.

The ideal trainer should be alert and vibrant and have a cheerful encouraging manner.
– Lee Priest and Kurtis Ray

There are lots of bodybuilders and fitness buffs that enjoy passing on their knowledge and the benefit of their experience to others. Some find that they get such satisfaction and fulfillment out of this that they decide to make it their profession. Many of these go into the gym business either as instructors, managers or gym owners, but many are now becoming personal trainers. As bodybuilding and body-awareness has grown, the demand for personal trainers has grown with it.

What does it take to be a personal trainer? Well, the first requirement is that you've got to look the part. This of course, is in order to inspire confidence in your pupils. Now by this, I don't mean that you need to look like a physique contest winner, but you should have a better than average physique and be in good firm shape. I know one trainer with a terrific physique who tells me that he has to wrap up well when visiting certain clients because his super muscularity gives them a complex. I mention this as I think it's important. Your pupil has to feel at home with you and not feel overshadowed or in any way uncomfortable. For this reason some of the most successful personal trainers are from the middleweight sector of the physical spectrum. The ideal trainer should be alert and vibrant and with a cheerful encouraging manner. If you are thinking of going into this field, there's one more quality that's very important, you need to be caring.

Above all, you'll need knowledge. If you have your sights set on becoming a personal trainer you've probably been training for three or four years at least, and you'll have read every printed word on health, fitness and muscle building that you can. You will have absorbed a mountain of information and it will stand you in good stead. So where do we go from here? Well, if you haven't already done so, I'd strongly advise enrolling in one of the certification courses advertised in the bodybuilding press. A good course of study will fill in the grey areas in your knowledge and refresh your memory on other subjects. In addition to this, you'll come away with proof that you know your stuff.

Models: Frank Cassavetes and Ricardo Avala   Photo courtesy of Gold's Gym, Venice, CA

Your pupil has to feel at home with you and not feel overshadowed or in any way uncomfortable.

Once you have the certificate under your belt you'll be ready to go out and face the world. Some of the better courses on the market give you advice on how to do this. They also show you how to run the business side of things, such as price structure and presentation. This is very important. It pays to listen to the voices of experience.

You can start off as small as you like. Once you have your first two or three clients and if you do your job properly, the word will spread. You may need to do some local advertising to increase your clientele. Many trainers started out as part-time operators later to find that the demand forced them to go full time. They are not complaining.

You needn't limit your scope to bodybuilding and fitness alone, there are other activities which fit in very well. There are courses available on nutrition, stress management and fitness therapy. These make excellent second strings. Many trainers also do massage. This means that you've got to lug that treatment table around, but there are some very good lightweight folding models on the market.

Many clients seek their personal trainers' advice and guidance when equipping a home gym. Trainers, because of their connections within the field, usually have good relations with dealers and suppliers of equipment and are often able to secure good discounts. This can be of mutual benefit to both the trainer and his pupil. Though it may entail the trainer doing a little extra leg work, it is worthwhile.

Lots of people dream that one day they'll open a gym, but very often the idea has to be put on hold, owing to lack of funds. If you are one of these people, you may be considering doing a stint as a personal trainer, in order to boost your bank balance. It has one advantage over the gym idea in that it doesn't take any capital to get you started and in fact, it will generate some. At the same time it's a means of gaining experience, which will be invaluable when you do open your own gym. If you build up a good following, it should produce some founder members. It would also mean that you would open your gym with a ready-made reputation.

– Gordon Lavelle and
Andrew Pace

Though it's true that most of the personal trainers' clients are seen in their own homes, there is also lots of scope for gym training. In this situation the trainer and his pupil use a convenient gym. Most gym owners are prepared to co-operate on this, after all, if the trainer brings along a client that gym wouldn't otherwise have had, the operator has nothing to complain about.

Training your clients in a gym has its advantages over home training. The main benefit is that you'll have a much wider range of equipment at your disposal, unless you client is a millionaire with a fabulous poolside home-gym set up. The extra equipment means a much more varied exercise diet and so it's easier to keep the client happy and satisfied.

There is a growing trend toward gym operators employing personal trainers to give one-on-one instruction to some of their members. This kind of service is offered as an extra, of course, but it creates more demand for personal trainers. For the trainer himself, he will gain much insight into the business side of things through actually working in the gym environment. Such experience is invaluable to anyone contemplating eventual gym ownership.

There are alot of opportunities in this relatively new branch of the fitness industry. As with gym management it is entirely made up of men and women from within the health and fitness movement. Enthusiasts who make their living spread their enthusiasm.

Much of the information and advice given in this book is applicable to the personal training field, particularly chapters 5,11 and 12.

There is a growing trend toward gym operators employing personal trainers to give one-on-one instruction to some of their members. — Thomas Zechmeister

Advertising and Publicity

Advertising and publicity are essential to success in business. The health industry is no exception, because of the nature of the business a gym needs a constant flow of new members.

It is a sad fact but it's got to be faced, the dropout rate is high. Time and time again you will have seen beginners start out full of enthusiasm. They may tell everybody that it's the best thing they have ever done (possibly true) and that their only regret is not having started earlier. Yet in a couple of months they've disappeared. Gone! And not a word of explanation. Not to worry, once they have gone there's not much that can be done about it.

Why is the dropout rate so high? It's difficult to say. Some gave up when they didn't get the results they expected overnight. Others convinced themselves that it was too much like hard work. Sometimes love life or domestic life interferes. Who knows? Once they have gone you can't ask the reason why. The fact is, they have to be replaced. To do this you have to advertise.

The Media

Advertising comes in various shapes and sizes. Newspapers, magazines, television, local radio stations, local movie houses and posters come to mind immediately. Some forms of advertising are well suited to our particular needs and some are not. Fortunes have been misspent on advertising. Your advertising has to be done, not only in the right place, but also at the right time. More about the timing later, first let us look at some of the advertising media.

Advertising and publicity are essential to success in business. – Danielle Vece

Unfortunately, advertising on the radio or television is too expensive and must be ruled out.

• Newspapers

The press is one of the most efficient means of getting your message across to the public, as far as our business is concerned. However, the actual papers that you decide to use have to be chosen with some care. The national papers, are not for the average sized gym operator. Their rates are very high. They count their circulation in millions, but as they are spread out from the Rockies to the Rio Grande, there's too much wastage. If you happen to be the owner of a nationwide chain of health studios, with branches in various towns, it's a different story.

If your gym is in a large city, your local daily paper would be the best choice to advertise in. It directly serves the people in your catchment area and has lower advertising rates than national papers. Smaller local weekly papers may have lower advertisement rates but may not be as cost effective. Due to the weekly paper having smaller circulation, the extra expenditure of the daily would produce better results. The clientele of the health and fitness industry comprises a small part of the community.

The idea of advertising is to let the public know that your gym or centre exists and also to tell them where it is. This is particularly important if you are in a big city. City folk are too busy to know what's going on, even if it's happening just around the corner. You've got to tell them and you've got to tell them again and again.

Newspaper advertising can prove very effective, but only in big circulation papers. Avoid small specialized periodicals, even though their rates seem very much cheaper. Don't forget that every policeman who reads the "Police Gazette" and every teacher who read "Education Weekly," also reads the daily papers – and so do millions more. Why not reach these as well?

• Magazines

The mass circulation national magazines give rise to the same problem as the national newspapers – wastage. Like the national dailies their rates can be prohibitively high and are therefore best left alone.

Physical culture magazines, taken at face value, seem to be an obvious choice and their rates are much cheaper than the more general interest journals. However one must bear in mind a couple of points:

• You will be "preaching to the converted." Most of the people reading your ads will already be aware of the value of physical culture and exercise. More often than not they will also be members of a gym or sports centre.

• As with other magazines, they are distributed nationwide, so much of the readership lives hundreds of mile away, so there is a lot of wasted coverage.

Now this doesn't mean that you shouldn't advertise in the muscle and fitness magazines. So by all means do, as their rates are usually reasonable. However, don't expect fantastic results. Remember too, that these magazines need your support. They give invaluable publicity and support to the physical culture movement itself and as a gym operator you are part of this movement.

Keep in mind the fact that publicity in these magazines, in the form of a write-up, or editorial coverage is very valuable. An editor is much more likely to give you a mention, or a couple of paragraphs, if you advertise in his magazine occasionally.

• Radio and Television

These media must be ruled out because of cost.

• Local Cinemas

Great for the Chinese restaurant or the Pizzeria that's just across the road from the cinema, but no good for the gym business. Cinema audiences are too small; we need to deal in thousands rather than hundreds.

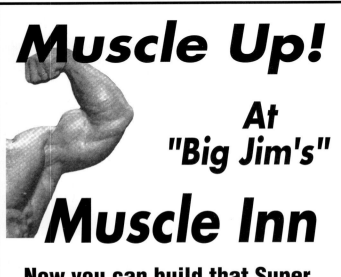

Muscle Up!

At "Big Jim's"

Muscle Inn

Now you can build that Super Physique with "Big Jim" Orlando Masses of Hi-Tech equipment and TONS of heavy metal

Work out with the champions

36 Main Street, Bedrock. Tel 9769754

• Posters

Used wisely posters can be very effective. Often it's easy to get them displayed in sports shops and health food stores; they can hardly refuse when you point out that you share some of the same clientele. Offer to reciprocate with their poster in your place. Perhaps in addition, you can come to an arrangement on some of their products.

Personally, I found poster advertising on the platforms and passageways of the subway system, very productive. I used only the busiest downtown stations. The rates are higher for these extra busy stations and though this advertising was expensive it also proved to be very cost effective. This of course, is entirely due to the huge numbers of people who use the subway stations every day.

In smaller cities and towns, where there is no subway, there will be poster sites which can be used to great advantage. These are usually handled by local publicity and advertising agencies. Sometimes these agencies handle not only the booking of sites, but can also deal with artwork and printing.

The usual poster size for this kind of advertising is what the printers call a 20" x 30". By the skillful use of two colors, say black and red, a good, eye-catching effect can be achieved. It is a mistake to crowd a poster with too much lettering. The advertising men tell us that white space sells – and so it does. If you leave plenty of white background, your message stands out more and it will have greater impact.

**The "Ladies Only" Gym
that has everything**

**Slimming, Aerobics, Fitness,
Bodybuilding, Jacuzzi, Sauna,
under the personal direction of**

ANNE GODDARD

22 The Albany, Clifton. Tel 723 709965

Keep your message brief. It is essential to get across who you are, where you are and what you offer. Make sure your telephone number is big and bold. You will probably use some form of illustration on your posters, human figures or silhouettes. It is important that these look like people and not monsters. I have seen otherwise good advertising and masthead logos spoiled by the inclusion of grotesque caricatures that would make Arnold Schwarzenegger look like an anorexic choirboy. Many would-be members are put off by the sight of super-Herculean muscularity, they shy away if they think your place is full of these giants. Depict muscularity by all means, but keep it pleasingly athletic looking.

In addition to the two color 20 x 30s, it's a good idea to have some smaller posters or notices, say A4 size. These are useful and can be sited strategically. Sympathetic shopkeepers are often willing to display one. Unlike the larger posters there is practically no real cost involved, if you have access to a computer and/or a scanner, or even a photocopier. They can be in one color and it doesn't call for any special skills to get a good effect.

• **Brochures**

A good attractive-looking brochure, depicting your set-up and what it has to offer, may on first thoughts seem almost a necessity. It isn't necessarily so. Getting them designed and printed can be quite expensive. Distribution too, can be a costly process and it is very difficult to check that whoever is supposed to be shoving them into mailboxes is actually doing the job. You have no proof that your precious brochures have not found their way into a convenient trash can.

Brochures are, of course, tailor made for distribution by post, but bear in mind that this also add to the initial outlay and also that many people have an aversion to junk mail and much precious artwork goes straight into the garbage.

Occasionally someone will stick his head around the door of the gym and ask for a brochure. You give him one and he scurries off. It's almost a certainty that you'll never see him again. I have experimented with this situation by saying, "Sorry, we haven't any brochures at the moment, but if you'd like to come in, I'll show you around and explain everything." The result of this little speech is quite predictable.

You find he's in "rather a hurry" or he's double-parked and he'll call in again. He can't get out quick enough. So why did he come in in the first place? Perhaps a psychiatrist could throw some light on this phenomenon.

GYMBIZ

Though I hate to sound negative, in the end I am forced to say that in my opinion brochures shouldn't be used. There are, fortunately, other far more effective ways of spending your advertising budget.

Newspaper Advertising

Let's return to newspaper advertising, because that is where the greater part of your advertising budget will be spent.

Having chosen the paper, or papers, that you are going to use, you have to decide on the size and type of your ads. The larger display advertisements, in which you pay according to column space, naturally have more impact than smaller lineage ads, which are charged based on the number of lines or words.

To launch a new venture it's well worth going for display adver-

tising, you need to start off with maximum impact. With newspaper display ads, the same rules apply as with poster advertising, white space sells. Don't overcrowd your space with unnecessary wording. Make sure your telephone number stands out. Once you're business is up and running, you will probably find that smaller ads in the classified or personal columns will be sufficient, with the odd display ad from time to time.

If you are in a small to medium sized town you may find that, after a while your advertisements lose some of their pulling power. You can spread the effect of this saturation by alternating between two newspapers, if there are two available. Occasionally, you may have to give the newspaper medium a short rest.

Seasons

There is a right and wrong time to advertise and the reason for this is simple. The health and fitness field is divided into several seasons. There are times of the year when people start to think about doing something about their physical well-being and bodily shape. These are, if you like, the high seasons of the gym world. These are the times when the gym suddenly gets busier than usual. Old members who have missed a couple of months, suddenly turn up again, but more important, new ones start to come in through the door. And, if your advertising is doing its job, the telephone starts to ring.

In contrast, you have the low seasons when business just goes flat. There are practically no beginners starting and even some of the old regulars don't turn up.

The High Seasons:

• New Years

This starts immediately after the holiday, on the second of January. This is when, spurred on by New Year resolutions, new people flock to the gym. The rush lasts about a month and then things settle down.

• First breath of Spring

This starts when people begin to think that summer is not too far away and it's time to do something about their condition. It begins in April and lasts about three months.

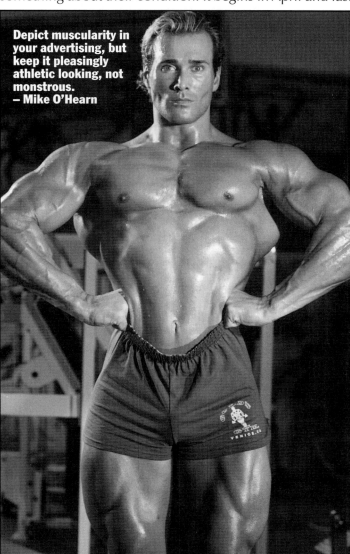

Depict muscularity in your advertising, but keep it pleasingly athletic looking, not monstrous.
– Mike O'Hearn

• The Fall

There is always an influx of beginners during September and it carries on well into October. Probably due to people making up their minds while on holiday, that they really must do something about the flab.

The Low Seasons:

These are the times when very few people seem to be interested in starting to improve their bodies and many of those who have started seem to find other things to do. Fortunately there are only two of these troughs. They arrive like clockwork every year and there is nothing we can do to alter this.

• Mid July thru August

In the United States, as in Europe in general, mid July to the end of August is peak vacation time. It is quite natural that there is a fall off in gym attendance. If you are in a holiday resort, or a tourist centre, you may get the odd visitor who wants the odd workout. Apart from this it's a fairly dead period.

• December

Once it is sensed that Christmas is in the air, everybody seems to banish all thoughts of physical betterment. The Christmas fever starts on December first and becomes worse as the month progresses. There are almost no joiners or enquirers. It will also be noted that many of the dyed-in-the-wool regulars fail to turn up. What to do? Sit tight, or take a holiday, the New Year rush is just around the corner.

Timing Your Advertising

There is nothing that can be done to alter the above seasons, the low ones that is. A barrage of advertising during the quiet months won't help; it's just like throwing money down the drain. On the other hand, to make the most of your advertising, you must do the bulk of it during the peak months. This is the time when there are people out there ready to bite.

Publicity

Publicity usually comes free, but it sometimes needs a little effort and legwork to get it. You have to make sure that you get the maximum mileage out of it. Let me explain.

Suppose you have arranged for some well-known personality or sportsman to be photographed by the press at your gym. When the journalist and photographer arrive you get their assurance that they will mention the name of your gym when the piece is published. They will agree to this, but don't be too disappointed if, when you see the paper the following day, you find they've forgotten to mention your gym by name. I really don't know why the press has

To make the most of your advertising, you must do the bulk of it during the peak months.
– Jeff Poulin

T-shirts with your gym's name on it are an excellent way to advertise.
– Lee Priest

this reluctance to say just which gym figures in their photograph, but you can be sure that Mr. Personality gets his name in and spelled correctly too.

I experienced this a couple of times before I devised a plan to beat it. I had "Ravelle's Health Centre" painted on the wall inside the gym. All I had to do then was to make sure that "Jack the Lad" was photographed in a position where my artwork was in the background.

Another useful ploy is to have the person wear one of the gym's tee shirts. If he's got the gym's name boldly emblazoned on his chest, you can't fail.

Collaboration with fairs, bazaars and other events in your district means good exposure. Make sure that you get mentioned in all their publicity and posters etc.

As mentioned earlier, a write-up in any of the physical culture or health journals is always good publicity and not too difficult to come by. The editors of these magazines are always looking for something new and interesting in the way of copy. If, for example, you've got an up and coming young bodybuilding hopeful training at your gym, a short piece on him with a photograph, is almost an offer that can't be refused.

When dealing with physical culture and health magazines, don't forget that the subject of your publicity doesn't necessarily have to be a bodybuilder or athlete. Editors are equally, or sometimes even more interested, if you have some well-known personality, from some other field, among your members. In these cases a photograph is a must, but usually the celebrity is delighted to collaborate.

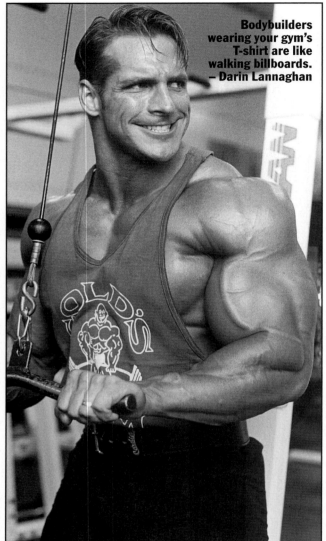

Bodybuilders wearing your gym's T-shirt are like walking billboards. – Darin Lannaghan

Word of Mouth

Recommendation is the best form of publicity that you can have and it doesn't cost anything. If you treat your members well, make sure they get good results and you give good service, they'll tell their friends. A new prospect that's brought in by a friend is much, much better than one who has just walked in off the street. You have very little selling to do; his friend has already sold him on the idea. Some gyms offer incentives, like a month's free membership, for people bringing say, two new members in one month. This and similar ideas can help swell your ranks.

Stickers

Windshield stickers are a good means of showing the flag and once you've printed them, distribution comes free of charge, your members do the job for you. I have found them to be most effective and a good investment. Hand them out to as many of your members as possible.

Through trial and error I found that the best size is about four inches in diameter. If they are too large some of the more car-proud members don't like to display them, but the discreet four or five inch disc seems to please everybody.

T-Shirts

There is good advertising and publicity value in the printed t-shirt and there is always a demand for them. Use bold lettering that will catch attention and if you use figures, my advice is keep away from those grotesque, over-muscular giants. This type of artwork will appeal to your hardcore members, but lots of the others may shy away.

You will need to stock three or four sizes of tee shirts and at least as many colors. A white t-shirt offers the greatest contrast to the color of the lettering. White t-shirts tend to become dirty and stained faster than a bold color. If the t-shirt gets messy and stained, people will wear it less and reduce the exposure of your advertisement. I think it's best to use red, blue or yellow.

As an advertising media the t-shirt is pretty good. I remember a young lady telling me that she had joined the gym after stopping a boy in the street, in a busy coastal resort, and copying the telephone number, which was displayed on his chest. There is more about t-shirts in the chapter on peripherals.

The old expression "It pays to advertise" is true, but only if the advertising is in the right place and at the right time.

Lee Priest

The Telephone

The results of good advertising and publicity can be judged immediately by the increased telephone activity. The calls that you get in answer to your ads are precious, treat each one with special care. The next thing you've got to concentrate on is getting those callers to actually come into the gym. "Butts through the door" is what we're after. If you handle these calls in the right manner, a high percentage of the callers will come through the door. If your telephone technique is not up to scratch, you'll be losing potential business. All you've got to do is remember a few simple points and it will make all the difference.

After greeting the caller, ask how you can help, what exactly is he or she interested in. You can start by saying something like, "Oh, we can certainly help you there." And continue by naming what facilities you have and what hours and days you are open. At this juncture let me bring up two very important points:

Models: Maurice Murphy and Scott Baur   Photo courtesy of Gold's Gym, Venice, CA

Remember that your telephone is your lifeline. It's your link with the outside world and with your advertising. It must always be free for incoming calls, so it's a good idea to have a payphone for the use of members and staff.

1. Try to avoid discussing prices and rates over the phone.

2. Don't give away too much information over the phone. If you tell the caller too much at this stage, particularly if you mention your rates, you may satisfy his curiosity and this gives him less reason for making a personal visit. If you have talked about charges, you will have left the caller free to decide whether or not to join, without his seeing the facilities and what you have to offer. If he decides not to join without even seeing the place, you have not given yourself an even chance.

If possible you should remain in control of the conversation and lead it from stage to stage. One of the best ploys is, after starting as above, when you've mentioned the opening hours etc., you say, "Of course it's very difficult on the phone, why don't you come in and you can see exactly how things work?" The caller will probably agree and you can go ahead and fix a time. Try to do this for the same day if possible. Same day appointments have a much better chance of turning up than those made for the following day.

It has been found that one of the best methods of getting the caller to agree on a time for the appointment, is to offer two distinct times of the day. Something like, "I can see you at three o'clock this afternoon, or seven this evening ... which suits you best?" (Note the "I can see you" bit. This suggests that you're busy, but you'll fit the caller in just the same.) Usually the prospect will either accept one of the two times, or come up with an alternative and you make the appointment. All you have to do then, is sit back and wait to see if the prospect turns up.

The caller may of course, give you that old well-worn, "Well, I'm a bit tied up right now, but I'll get back to you" routine. That's too bad, there's not a lot you can do and you have little option but to go along with it. Do not counter by getting too pushy on the matter of this appointment. This smacks too much of high-pressure sales talk and must be avoided at all costs if you want to keep your good name.

Give clear, concise directions to callers, so that they can find your place without too much trouble. It is very helpful if you can give directions from a well-known landmark or building. Work out your own telephone procedure, based on the above and on your own local geography. Have any members of your staff who may answer the telephone, memorize this procedure.

Remember that your telephone is your lifeline. It's your link with the outside world and with your advertising. It must always be free for incoming calls, so it's a good idea to have a payphone for the use of members and staff.

"If a man builds a better mousetrap, the world will beat a path to his door." The expression is part of America's industrial folklore. Henry Ford knew about it in his day and Bill Gates knows it's just as true today.

The Mousetrap Theory applies to most businesses, but the fitness industry is just that little bit different and we need a slightly different approach. We need to study people's behavior, attitudes and ways of thinking and we have to apply the findings in order to gain new converts to our way of life.

The telephone is very often where you will make your first acquaintance with a prospective new member. Usually it is the caller's first contact with, what he may see as, an entirely new way of life. Much may depend on that first tentative phone call. It is as important that you create a good impression, as it is that you get the caller to come in through the door.

The gym business is a challenging way of life, but it can also be very rewarding and fulfilling. In any business, one of the most important ingredients for success is belief in what you're selling. You must be a believer or you wouldn't be reading this book.

The Peripherals

There are many interesting sidelines or additional activities that can be combined with our mainstream bodybuilding and fitness business. Some of these are often provided simply as an extra service to the members. Others can be, in themselves, quite lucrative. Which of these peripheral activities the gym owner decides to incorporate, may of course, depend largely on space and time available.

Food Supplements

Since the American muscle mogul, Joe Weider first launched his protein tablets and Crash Weight powder back in the early fifties, the bodybuilding food supplement field has grown into a giant industry employing an army of intelligentsia. These chemists, scientists and PhD's are all striving to upgrade and increase the efficiency of their magic potions and powders. This has brought about great progress in nutritional science and this reflects in the quality of the physiques seen in present day athletes and bodybuilders.

Food supplements are a great sideline that takes up little or no space and time. It creates a service for the members and it is a growing market. Today there are lots of manufacturers who are eager to supply these products and usually they offer a very good delivery service.

You need not carry a large stock if you are dealing with a supplier who can give you rapid service. This means that you don't need to have a large amount of capital tied up on your shelf.

Model: Robert Delariva

Food supplements create a service for the members and it is a growing market.

A juice bar won't lead to big money, but it is a service.

A shelf, or better still a lockable showcase, is all the space you need. Due to the advertising of the manufacturers in the physical culture press, these products largely sell themselves. Having recommendations by satisfied users helps and creates a snowball effect.

While the average gym operator is not going to get rich selling amino acids, vitamins and weight-gaining tablets, he should at least be able to offset the electricity and telephone bills.

Juice Bar

People get thirsty when working out, so a juice bar makes sense. You can sell canned, bottled or fresh fruit juices. You can also mix your own house health drink using fruit juice or milk and protein powder. Be sure that you stock sugar-free drinks for the benefit of the weight conscious. The wall behind the bar is a good place to have your display of food supplements, thus killing two birds with one stone.

Again, a bar won't lead to big money, but it is a service. Some gym owners give the bar concession responsibility to one of the staff, usually an instructor. He supplies his own stock and he keeps the profits, for him it's an extra perk.

Some establishments, usually larger ones, prefer to have the bar "nationalized." They may, or may not give the staff a percentage of the takings.

T-Shirts, Tank Tops and Training Gear

Sports and gym wear bearing your gym name or logo is always saleable, so this is another avenue to be explored. More important it's great publicity too, when you have people parading around with your name on their chests.

You can buy the garments wholesale and then have a printer do the rest, he will work from artwork that you have to supply, or he may have his own artist who will produce the artwork from your own rough sketch.

The main problem here can be cash flow. In order to get a good price on the goods and even more so on the printing, you have to order in bulk. You have to think in hundreds rather than dozens. This means money that is tied up until the goods are sold.

GYMBIZ

Now, it's obvious that the more reasonable the price of your tee shirts the quicker you'll sell them and you will achieve quicker cash flow. If your main interest in the goods is their publicity value, then sell them at a bargain price, an "offer they can't refuse," you'll achieve two objectives. 1. You will be creating quick cash flow. 2. You will be getting your publicity out on the streets quickly. There is no advertising value if the shirts are left sitting on the shelf.

If publicity and advertising value are of secondary importance (hard to imagine) then you can, of course, hold out for a greater profit margin and a slower turnover. Personally I would settle for a middle-of-the-road plan. I'd sell cheaply but still with a little profit margin and look upon the advertising value as the rest of the profit.

Aerobics

In recent years the interest in aerobics has grown tremendously and this has brought more and more women into the gym scene. Many gym owners who previously only offered bodybuilding and fitness training were quick to climb on the bandwagon. Now it is becoming standard for any gym to have an aerobics section.

The requirements are anything from about 350 square feet and upwards, of clear smooth floor space and a good instructor. Bear in mind that aerobics classes are ninety-odd percent female and would prefer a female instructor.

The floor space, you either have it or you don't. The instructor? Well, this is where you've got to proceed with caution. Choose with great care. In any branch of the gym business the choice of the teacher is very important, but nowhere so much as in aerobics.

Your aerobics instructor has to have some very special qualities. If she's not right, she can decimate your class size in less than a month. I have seen it happen.

The interest in aerobics has grown tremendously and this has brought more and more women into the gym scene.

First and foremost she must know her stuff and must be dedicated to her discipline. She must also have a good trim figure. However, knowledge, ability and shape alone are not enough. Personality is of great importance, she must be lively and vibrant. Possessing strong leadership qualities is also important. Ideally, a charismatic person who will give her class a sense of purpose would be the best choice.

On the floor she must be able to maintain firm discipline and order without the harshness of a sergeant major. She must be able to show firmness and understanding.

In the early days of aerobics I engaged a young lady who had previously been a ballet teacher. Though dancers and ex-dancers usu-

Your aerobics instructor should be dedicated and know her stuff. – Brandi Carrier

ally make excellent aerobics teachers, in this case the results were disastrous. She turned out to be a harsh disciplinarian who hadn't realized that there's a vast difference in the abilities of a group of aerobics afficionados and a class of ten-year-old ballet students. The class just fell apart and Madame Dogsbody had to be replaced.

If at all possible, arrange to see her at work in front of a class. Failing this, try to get some idea of her suitability by asking around or by referring to people who have seen her in action and are in a position to comment.

The system of payment for aerobics instructresses varies. In some cases they are paid a flat hourly rate and in others they are paid a percentage, often 40 or 50 percent of the takings. Which system you go for will depend on various factors. The most obvious of these is class size. Percentage payment on a class of 30 will amount to double of that on a class of 15, yet the workload is not double. On the other hand, if a bigger class means more money, the teacher may see this as an incentive, which could be to the benefit of all. This is something that the management has to play by ear according to the circumstances.

Spinning, Body Pump and other Class Activities

Currently there is growing interest in class activities apart from aerobics. Amongst the new crazes are Body Pump and Spinning. Unlike aerobics they seem to appeal equally to both sexes.

GYMBIZ

In Body Pump the class performs weight training exercises to music, it is of course, a cardiovascular workout. In a Spinning class the group perform cycling to music. The size of the class is limited by the number of bikes and the amount of space available. Both these activities and one or two others have turned out to be money spinners. The two mentioned are licensed systems, but many operators have come up with their own systems and cut out the middleman.

As with aerobics, the choice of your instructor is vital and experience in exercise to music is essential.

Karate and Martial Arts

Karate, Tae kwon do and other martial arts fit in well with the fitness gym concept and like aerobics, all that you require is some clear floor space and an instructor. You can in fact, use the same floor space for both aerobics and martial arts. This is usually a question of alternating the days of the different activities, or juggling with the timetable.

Instructors, as in the case of aerobics, must be selected with care. Karate has become a cult, and you will find that the people who are attracted to it are quite different, for instance, from the people who come along to do bodybuilding, though there are of course, some who do both.

Choose carefully when hiring instructors. They must be lively and vibrant. – Vicky Pratt

In many cases a karate teacher may become something of a cult leader figure and will as a result, develop his own loyal following. An instructor with this type of charisma never lacks for students.

It is easy to see that in addition the instructor's personal ability as a karate instructor, personality and personal magnetism are very important. I had the good fortune and privilege to work with a dedicated group of Japanese instructors, headed by the world famous, seventh Dan, Tatsuo Suzuki. He and his team, all had the above mentioned qualities and our karate involvement grew to such proportions that we had to rent extra premises just to accommodate it.

Now, while it is true that we had the benefit of native Japanese teachers and this was one of the factors in our success, it is also true that an instructor doesn't have to be oriental to have that all important charisma. In fact, over a period of time we found that two or three of our own pupils, who had started with us as beginners, had the qualities, which later made them fine teachers.

In martial arts, as in other gym-type disciplines, the dropout rate, particularly in the early stages, is high. However, if you've got the right teacher or teachers, you can, to a degree, minimize this.

Karate, the masters tell us, is self-selective. That is to say, by its very nature it weeds out and discards those who are not really suitable to follow this path. I have my own way of interpreting this.

Many beginners take up karate for all the wrong reasons or, without really having any idea of what it's all about. Some think that within a few weeks they'll be able the thrash a vanload of hooligans single-handed. Others savor the idea of smashing an oak table with a single barehanded blow. There are also those who are impressed and lured by the Oriental mystique that surrounds all martial arts. Later when they find themselves marching up and down, punching thin air like regimented robots, they may begin to realize that karate is not quite what they thought it was. Doing pushups supported only by your knuckles isn't much fun. The training is tough and tiring and yet, in the early weeks there is not much real action and certainly no sign of combat. The dropout rate is high, but those that are still there after three or four months are likely to stay with it.

A good teacher is one who can hold his class, or most of it, together through this initial break-in period. Later, when things become more interesting, it's not so difficult.

There is good spin-off from karate. Many enthusiasts, realizing that they are lacking in physical strength, may combine karate with weight training. Conversely, you will find that some of your weight trainers add karate to their curriculum, in order to put their muscles to greater use.

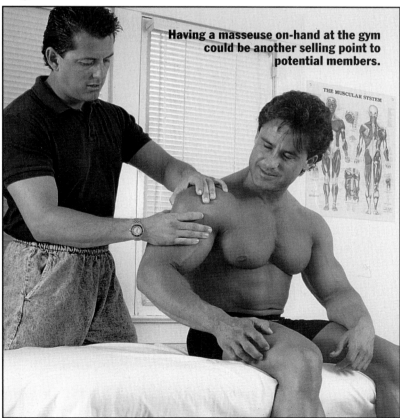

Having a masseuse on-hand at the gym could be another selling point to potential members.

Massage

Now here is something, which seems, at the very mention of the word, to fit in perfectly with gymnastic surroundings. However, if this is true, why is it that so many gyms don't have a masseur, or masseuse? I think there are far more massages done by practitioners visiting their clients at home, than there are in gyms. For one thing, many of the people who indulge in massage, do so in the belief that it is the answer to their weight problems. They are also the people who don't care to exert themselves in a gym. By the way, it's no good telling these people that the only person who loses weight through massage, is the masseur. You still won't get them to come to the gym.

GYMBIZ

Then there is the economical side of things. If the masseur sets up his table in a gym, the proprietor will expect a percentage of his takings or, some sort of rent. Whereas, if he sets up on his own, doing house calls, his only needs are a mobile phone and a portable table. He can charge more, for the convenience of home service and he pockets the lot. For this reason lots of people working as personal trainers have found it profitable to add massage to their menus as a sideline.

There are some gym operators who offer massage and do it themselves, thus cutting out the need to employ an extra person. This can work out well, but it can really only be confined to off peak hours, when the owner doesn't need to have his finger on the pulse. This time restriction itself, limits the amount of revenue brought in.

It may seem strange, but in the average gym or fitness centre, that has a masseur, there never seems to be as much business generated, as one would imagine. At the more expensive up-market establishments, it's a different story, but of course, you're dealing with a different type of clientele. They are the ones who can afford to pay for a little pampering.

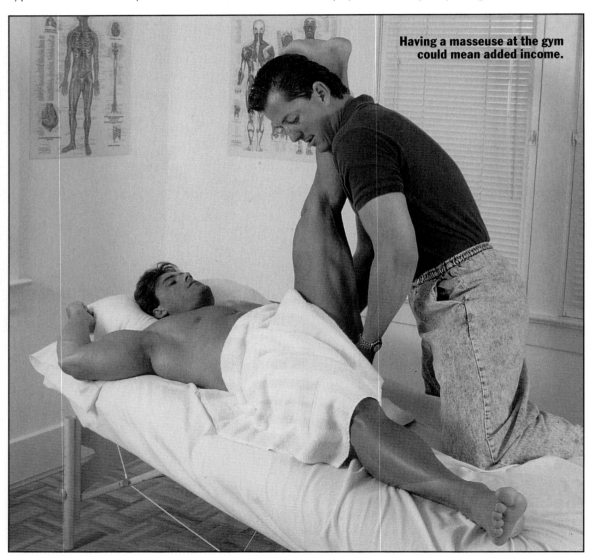

Having a masseuse at the gym could mean added income.

Sauna

I have included sauna in this list of peripheral activities, though some operators wouldn't consider it peripheral. Many gyms include the use of the sauna in their membership fees, at no extra cost. Whether or not an operator does this will depend on various factors.

If there is competition in the area and they are including sauna as part of their membership deal, he may feel he has to go along with it and do the same. On the other hand he may decide on a lower basic gym fee and charge for sauna as an extra. There's a good argument for this, as people who are not interested in sauna will be attracted by the lower price.

However, there is one point to bear in mind. If you are charging for sauna as an extra, you have to have some control over who uses it. If not the "gate crashers" will take advantage.

There are other sidelines, which can be complimentary to the gym business, but the ones listed here are the most common and those that are most compatible with the main activity, which is bodybuilding and fitness training.

Who wouldn't like to sit and relax in a sauna after a gruelling workout?
– Jay Cutler

Commercially, one of the greatest advantages weight training has over other gym activities, is that it's not done in class form and therefore the members are not tied to fixed hours to attend. This leads to a situation where you have an ever-changing group of people using the gym throughout the day. Obviously there will be peak hours when there are more people present and other times when there will only be two or three.

The fact that many members can train simultaneously at all hours of the day, generates the greatest revenue. Compare this with the floor space of a squash or raquetball court and revenue seems rather limited.

The astute operator will not lose sight of the fact that the main gym floor, with its bodybuilding and fitness facilities, is where his main interest must always lie. He must take this into consideration when contemplating other supplementary activities and diversifications.

Opening Day

You have been planning and scheming for a long time and at last you've got the whole thing together and you are ready to open your own studio. The question is how. Really there are two ways to do things and you have to decide which way you want to go.

1. Throw an opening party and open with a bang.
2. Simply open the doors and announce that you are ready for business.

This may at first, sound like a simple choice, but there are a few factors to consider. Let's take a closer look at these two completely different opening days.

Number one isn't really an opening day at all as you won't be open for normal business and there will be no-one training. Really it would be better described as a preview day. One thing is certain, people will arrive. People will turn up to anything that's free – especially if it

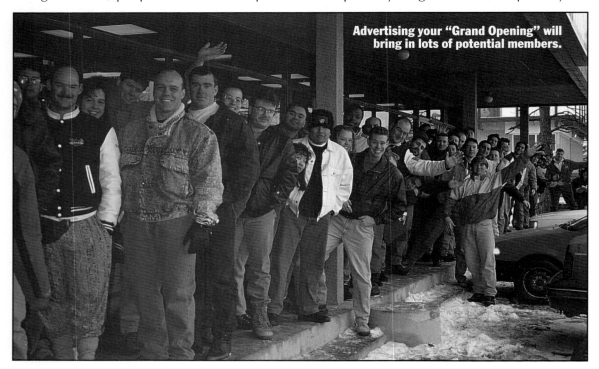

Advertising your "Grand Opening" will bring in lots of potential members.

Make sure to do one last inspection to make sure everything is in top shape.

involves food and drink of any kind. This creates the first drawback. Your place will be in a mess, even before you've opened. And don't forget that it's got to look absolutely pristine the following morning when you really open.

It's very difficult to tell people, who are not yet members, that they can't smoke on the premises and it's even more difficult to stop someone spilling drinks on your brand new carpet. However, apart from the mess and the unavoidable morning-after-the-night-before situation, think back. What is, or was, the real purpose of this opening party?

"Well," you may say, "the idea is to put the place on the map, let people know that we're here and sign up a few members."

Admittedly the above sounds like very good logic, but in practice things work out a little differently. The first two objectives you will achieve. The people that come to the party will know that you're there, so you will have put yourself on the map. However, you are going to find it very difficult to actually enroll members during party time.

As the host you'll be expected to be there, partying, mingling, and stopping children from killing or maiming themselves on the equipment. You will also have to stop some of the more stupid and extrovert of the adults from doing the same thing, because people love showing off on these occasions. When you get a chance you will be answering intelligent questions about the equipment and what its uses are. Not to mention the customers who grab two handfuls of midriff, (their own) and ask, "How do I get rid of this?"

Some of the guests will even remember to compliment you on how wonderful it all looks. In the midst of all this you may begin to realize that this is not the best time to even try to do business. That's a pity because it was the main reason for the party in the first place.

There is another drawback, all those people who came to the grand opening, perhaps 40 or 50 – maybe even a hundred – came, amongst other things, out of curiosity. Now this is good, you want people to be curious. The trouble is, that having been to the opening party they now know what your place is like and they have probably found out what your charges are. In other words their curiosity has been satisfied and many of them will never be seen again.

I attended an opening party recently, in fact, since I started writing this book. The new gym owner and his wife had labored long and hard to prepare everything for this reception and there was no shortage of guests. Mountains of sandwiches, biscuits, sausages on sticks and other junk food were consumed along with various beverages. In itself the party was a success.

A couple of weeks afterwards the owner admitted to me that it had not produced one client. He said the whole thing had been a lot of wasted time and effort. If all this sounds a little gloomy and negative let's have a look at the alternative.

Compare the above with option No. 2, the Not So Grand Opening. Having everything in a state of complete readiness, chromium plate and mirrors gleaming, you just open the front door.

You will, of course, have advertised in the press that you are opening today. Also you have put out some handbills to this effect and have a large Now Open sign displayed outside. The telephone will start to ring in answer to your newspaper ads and one or two at a time, people will start to come through the door.

All is quiet except for the muted music of your stereo system. It is the ideal atmosphere in which to show somebody around your facility, seat them in your office and discuss what you can do for them and give them the details of membership.

Fortunately, when any new gym opens, there are always a few people who can't wait to get started. Usually they have been, or are, attending another gym, but this one is closer, better, or whatever. They will have seen the preparations and know that a gym is opening. During the last week or so before the big day they put in frequent appearances, anxious to know the date. When they drift in on that first day they will expect to start training. This is fine, it adds a bit of background and shows that you really are up and running.

By the end of D-Day, despite any teething troubles that may have cropped up, you will have enrolled a few new members. The waiting and uncertainty are over and now you are ready to accept the challenges that come with any new business venture.

Now it's up to you to make sure that your project becomes a continuing success. Make sure that you and your staff are totally committed, this means that first and foremost you have to give the members the very best service possible.

It goes without saying that attention to the needs and problems of members on the gym floor has top priority. You and your staff are there to instruct, encourage and above all get results.

Always make sure that all equipment, not only in the gym but also in other areas such as showers and dressing rooms, is kept in tip-top condition. Try to keep the whole installation looking just as new and gleaming as it did on that first opening day.

What of the future? Never be complacent. Always be planning for your future growth and expansion. If you have any competition in your area you will have to try even harder to keep that one step ahead.

Yes, it's a great challenge, but it's well worthwhile.

Keep everything running in top condition and you'll not only have a successful business, but you'll have healthy and happy members for a long time to come.

Appendix
Most Frequently Asked Questions

Listed here are a dozen of the most frequently asked questions. These FAQ's, as the computer buffs call them, pop up with amazing regularity. Most of them have common-sense answers, though in some cases of course, the answer will depend on the exact circumstances. Nevertheless I have attempted to gener-alize.

Aaron Baker

Q – Is it better to do a few repetitions with a heavy weight or more reps with a lighter weight?
A – Well, it depends what your objective is and what you're trying to achieve. It is generally acknowledged that low reps, say three to six, are best for power and strength. Medium reps, eight to twelve, for building bulk and high reps, fifteen to twenty for reducing or definition training. This is not a hard and fast rule and varies from one individual to another. There are people who will gain bulk even on sets of twenty reps. Of course, a lot depends on diet. (At this point you have to stop generalizing and ask about the pupil's particular case.)

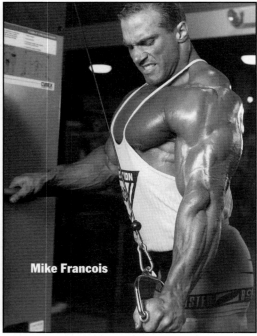

Mike Francois

Q – Can weight training make you muscle-bound?
A – No! And what do you mean by muscle-bound anyway? (The answers to this one are as priceless as they are varied.)

Q – What happens if I stop training. Does all the muscle turn to fat?
A – No. Fat and muscle are two different things and one cannot turn into the other. If you stop training you will lose some muscle size. You may put on some fat, if you have this tendency anyway. If you don't have this tendency you may even lose the odd pound as a result of the loss in muscle size.

Erikka Kern

Q – My wife wants to start training. Is there any danger that she will become overly muscular, like some of those girls I've seen in the muscle magazines?

A – The average woman responds well to weight training and the muscle will show as pleasing feminine curves, as women usually have thicker skin than men. The girls you are talking about are very special cases and usually have a tendency to muscular definition even before they start training. They also do a staggering amount of training. Those ladies didn't just get that way by accident. They have worked very hard and have achieved exactly what they wanted, though it may not appeal to everybody.

Q – I would like a bigger chest, should I do chest work every day?

A – No, if you did this your chest might become smaller. Muscles don't grow on the days that they are exercised, they grow on the rest days. Apart from the abdominals, no bodypart should be worked more than three times in a week. Some people get very good results on just two sessions per bodypart.

Q – Do I have to eat special foods to get good results from my training?

A – You will get good results from your training without following any special diet. That is to say just eating good wholesome food. However for maximum results what you eat is of the greatest importance. Despite this there have been champions who have thrived on fish and chips.

Q – Can I increase my height by exercise?

A – Not as far as I know, that is to say, I've never seen anybody do it, but it certainly won't have the reverse effect.

Brandi Carrier

Gunter Schlierkamp

Q – What do you think about these proteins and food supplements that are advertised in the magazines?

A – They are a good idea, especially if you are after maximum results. It's one way of making sure that you get the right ingredients in sufficient quantity. Bear in mind that food often loses much of its nutritional value in the cooking.

Q – Is it true that only the white of the egg should be eaten?

A – Many athletes eat only the white and throw away the yolk. It has been found that the yolk is where the cholesterol and saturated fat lurks. The white has no fat, much protein and it also contains anti-cholesterol bodies. Years ago we used to eat the yolk and throw away the white. This doesn't mean that you should never eat whole eggs. A healthy person on a relatively low-fat diet shouldn't have any problem eating up to three or four a week.

Q – I've heard that weights make you slow in other sports. Is this true?

A – No, there's no truth in this at all. Speed of movement depends on how quickly the brain can transmit messages to the muscles involved. Coaches and trainers the world over know this and that's why all the top athletes, including footballers and boxers, use weights in their training. Whatever your sport is, you'll play it better if you are stronger. Weights build power and strength.

Q – I am prone to lower back problems. Is it wise to do bodybuilding exercises with weights?

A – Yes, you can still practice bodybuilding, but there are certain exercises that you must avoid. Stiff leg deadlifts, Standing presses, Bent-over rowing motions, Good Morning exercises and heavy squats. There are other movements you can substitute for these. Machines are particularly useful in this area. We can also give you some special movements to strengthen the lumbar area.

Q – How many members do you have?

A – I left this one till the last because it's the most difficult to answer. Who is a member? Is it someone who has been coming to the gym for two years, someone who joined six months ago but hasn't been seen for six weeks, or someone who enrolled this very day? In truth any gym has a revolving membership and it is very difficult to estimate the actual size at any given time. If you try to explain all this it sounds as if you are being evasive, which is not the impression that you want to give. Without being untruthful, you will probably have some idea of how many people are using the place during an average week and you can quote this as your membership.

Lee Priest

Aaron Maddron

<u>Contributing Photographers</u>
Jim Amentler, Alex Ardenti, Reg Bradford, John A. Butler,
Gino Edwards, Skip Faulkner, Irvin Gelb, Chris Lund,
Jason Mathas, Steve Neece, Bert Perry, Dennis Warren